STUDIES IN
LOCAL HISTORY

Professor Winifred Maxwell

STUDIES IN LOCAL HISTORY

Essays in Honour of
Professor Winifred Maxwell

Edited by

J. A. BENYON   C. W. COOK

T. R. H. DAVENPORT   K. S. HUNT

Cape Town
OXFORD UNIVERSITY PRESS
London   New York
1976

Oxford University Press

OXFORD   LONDON   GLASGOW   NEW YORK
TORONTO   MELBOURNE   WELLINGTON   CAPE TOWN
IBADAN   NAIROBI   DAR ES SALAAM   LUSAKA   ADDIS ABABA
KUALA LUMPUR   SINGAPORE   JAKARTA   HONG KONG   TOKYO
DELHI   BOMBAY   CALCUTTA   MADRAS   KARACHI

*The authors acknowledge with thanks
the generous subsidy provided by
Rhodes University*

ISBN 0 19 570090 2

Printed by Citadel Press, Polaris Road, Lansdowne, Cape

CONTENTS

WINIFRED MAXWELL, HISTORIAN

Humour and humanity have distinguished the teaching of Winifred Maxwell. In the liberal tradition of Renaissance humanism (*non trascurando* Machiavelli!) she has been both a universal and extraordinarily diverse scholar; truly a 'Woman for all seasons'. But the Oxonian and English cast of her mind has also tempered 'Renaissance exuberance', for she would be the first to acknowledge her debt to distinguished mentors like Sir Maurice Powicke, Sir David Keir, V. H. Galbraith, and, beyond them, to the tradition of Maitland, Gardiner, and Stubbs (the Bishop, not Tommy!). So an Oxford emphasis on logic and accuracy, as much as Italianate inspiration, has accompanied Winifred Maxwell to the academic (and other) frontiers she has fought upon – and what a 'Bonnie Fechter', in the Rhodes Vice-Chancellor's words, she has proved!

Winifred Alice Maxwell (née Pronger) was born in London in 1907. She received her schooling at the Mary Datchelor Intercollegiate, which is renowned for the excellence of its products. Here she seems to have made an early impact, for she herself likes to recall that her school report once remarked 'Winnie is trying'!

Whatever the implications of this enigmatic comment, results speak for themselves, for the young Winifred proceeded to Oxford with an impressive array of scholarships to her credit: the Clothworkers' Company Exhibition, the Senior Open Scholarship to St. Hugh's College (the Clara Evelyn Morden Scholarship), a State Scholarship, and the London County Council Major Scholarship. This was followed by the award of a scholarship from the Goldsmiths' Company. The last is known to be her particular pride, for it is open to all undergraduates; and she still enjoys receiving an invitation to the Company's annual cocktail party.

A First Class Honours Degree in the School of Modern History crowned Winifred Maxwell's undergraduate career at Oxford. Her scholarships were renewed so that she might proceed to a research degree. Accordingly, in January 1932, she received the B.Litt. for her thesis on 'Thomas Gascoigne's Loci e Libro Veritatum'. Shortly afterwards she began reading for the Diploma in Education, which was predictably awarded with distinction in both the Theory and Practice of Education.

Armed with these impressive qualifications, the youthful academic set out to make her career. This was no easy undertaking for a woman in the depression years of the 'thirties. She taught first at the Parkfield Cedars School in Derby (1932–4) and, second, as senior history mistress at the Putney High School for Girls (1934–8).

In 1938 Winifred married James Maxwell and in the next year followed her husband to Rhodes University, Grahamstown, where he had an appointment in the Department of Psychology. Her son, Thomas, was born in 1942. As a wife and a mother she was clearly immersed in domestic concerns, but there was also a war on. In the temporary absence of Professor Michael Roberts on active service she acted as head of the Department of History at Rhodes for two years (1943 and 1944). Thus began her long association with the teaching of History in Southern Africa.

At the end of the war Winifred Maxwell returned temporarily to the United Kingdom, to Edinburgh; but she soon accepted a contract appointment at Rhodes while Michael Roberts was on study leave (1947–9). In 1952 she returned permanently to South Africa where she took up the post of Senior Lecturer in History and Political Science at the University of Natal. She moved back to Rhodes in July 1953 and was appointed to the Chair of History, in succession to Professor Roberts, in January 1954.

When Professor Maxwell retired from this Chair which she had filled with so much distinction, she was characteristically modest and generous in valediction: 'This has always been a good department, and I have merely built onto sound foundations'. For 21 years, until December 1974, she directed the development of the Department. Student numbers increased from 75 to over 200. Staff numbers, too, went up – from three to seven. Quite apart from achievements in teaching and research over this period, her administrative ability in accommodating these growing numbers within the departmental framework and in mounting the necessary new courses won the admiration of her colleagues and the university. As a member of the Library Committee from 1954 to 1974, she also developed the History section of the library to a point where its holdings are second to none in South Africa.

Apart from her years of work on Senate, Faculty, and Committee, Winifred Maxwell also served on the University Council and as Public Orator. In her inaugural lecture she quoted from Collingwood's Essay on Metaphysics: 'When Rome was in danger, it was the cackling of the sacred geese that saved the Capitol. I am only a professional goose, consecrated with cap and gown . . . but cackling is my job, and cackle I will'. Thus modestly she served advanced notice of some of the most brilliant public speaking and felicitous use of the spoken word that congregations of Rhodes University have yet heard.

After publishing on Thomas Gascoigne in the *English Historical Review* 1938–1939, she began to focus her own research interests on Southern Africa. To the *Encyclopaedia Britannica* she contributed a series of articles on the Cape, Natal, O.F.S., Transvaal, and Zululand. Her spadework then revealed much of the foundations of local regional history in the Eastern Province of the Cape of Good Hope. She presided over the writing of histories of Grahamstown and Graaff-Reinet and of the changing moods and shifting currents of provincial separatism. She garnered much valuable source material, both of British and local origin, relevant to the 1820 Settlers. Indeed, she developed a consuming interest in and unrivalled knowledge of these hardy pioneers. For her they were not only part of the diaspora of turbulent Regency Britain, but also a component of a local frontier interaction, whose dynamics, on both sides, she investigated and understood. Long before the modern schools of African History had changed the general emphasis of scholarship on the southern sub-continent, Winifred Maxwell's teaching was anticipating the main trend of their detailed research. Nor is her own contribution to this subsequent more intensive study a small one. Thanks to her sleuthing and supervision, critical editions of several diaries written on the 'interacting' frontier have seen the light of day. Her initiative has brought forward valuable evidence on settlement within this frontier of Xhosa-speaking *Mfengu*. She has broadcast on Cape editors, newspapers, and South African diaries, and her famous Dugmore Memorial Lecture, 'Reconsiderations', remains a gem for all Settler historians. Currently she is occupied in editing the Diary of Thomas Stubbs.

Perhaps her frontier life – not only in Grahamstown, but also upon the Caledonian 'Celtic Fringe', in Edinburgh – explains her love of the local. 'Why does Professor Maxwell hide her light under a bushel, so far from the centre of things?' a great historian of Southern Africa asked one of the editors. Surely the answer must be that she found the right stimulus to her talents on the periphery. To the edge of empire (as it was in 1939) she brought her intellectual diversity and there shared it generously with the hundreds who now, as essayists, editors, or edified students, offer this *Festschrift* in recognition.

In her adopted land Winifred Maxwell's range of expertise never left her at a loss to develop the particular interest of her students. As testimony, there is the sheer range of subject material in the essays of this collection. While she was ever master of what Hazlitt called 'the grand swirling movements of history' – those macrocosmic processes by which nations, religions, empires, and civilizations rise and fall – it was the microcosmic, the 'grass-roots' origins of those processes that seemed really to fire her enthusiasm. Invariably her stress on the interplay between centre and circumference, the percolation and capillarity between summit and substratum, gave relief to the researcher and inspiration to the uninspired. To them she would point out how the influences of the local and particular so often pass into the broad generalizations of national and international life. And, if they could not be proved to do so, the diversion into the *cul-de-sac* would be justified with the chuckle: 'At least you have established the negative, laddie!' Or, if she was in more sombre mood, her justification would be Bacon's defence of learning, which

> taketh away the wildness and barbarism and fierceness of men's minds; it taketh away all levity, temerity and insolency by copious suggestions of all doubts and difficulties and acquainting the mind to balance reasons on both sides, and to turn back the first offers and conclusions of the mind and to accept nothing but the examined and the tried . . . for of knowledge there is no satiety.

Such are the precepts by which Professor Maxwell has worked. It is therefore characteristic that she did *not* establish a school of specialized historians at Rhodes – though the postgraduate researches that she supervised, especially into the impact of British Colonial institutions upon South Africa's diverse peoples, may appear to many to amount to such a school. Equally expert in the fields of African, British, Mediaeval, Renaissance, European, Imperial, Colonial, and Modern History (and others, such as Arab and Chinese, that she pursued as 'hobbies'), she yet tended to eschew the regional and episodic: perhaps they were both too big and too small to suit her. If history is, at one level, a rich interweave of 'innumerable biographies', as she has argued, it deserves the magnifying glass – like the meticulous editing that she has devoted over the years to the Diary of Thomas Stubbs. If, on another level, it is the total sum of human experience, there is her caveat that the lens of the specialist may distort: the worm's eye, vital at the ground, is no substitute for the bird's eye. So Professor Maxwell has left behind her a legacy of attitudes, rather than a Rhodes school of history. Upon it she is no doubt content to be judged – and has been judged. At the Fourth Biennial Conference of the South African Historical Society the President, Professor Noel Garson, gallantly accorded her the accolade of 'doyen of modern South African historians' in recognition of her contribution to the scholarship of this country – and to those countries where her students have migrated. It is therefore the belief of the editors that their selection of 'Local History' as theme for this generalized collection of essays is consistent with the attitudes to history that Winifred Maxwell has sought to communicate.

There is another reason for choosing 'Local History' as focus of this tribute. Like all great teachers in the tradition of Socrates and Abelard, Winifred Maxwell has revelled in disputation: no fool was ever suffered gladly; but no serious student, however callow his understanding, failed to have his say or to 'follow the argument where it led'. Patience, logic, an unforced Socratic sequence – these were her path to the truth. But no one who has known her either as teacher, university professor, or housewife has remained unaware of the deep fund of rational and religious idealism that infuses her character. Laziness and mental sloth are her bane; her watchword is 'Freedom' – the freedom she has conceded to others to differ; the freedom she has in turn asserted to be different. 'Thinkers of the world unite,' she once adjured her students, 'You have nothing to lose but your brains!' Furthermore, she has always implied that these solid 'yeoman' qualities of independent thought and action spring from the conscious shouldering of responsibilities, however small, rather than from schools of abstract political or academic speculation. In the words of her favourite prayer from Chesterton:

> From all that terror teaches,
> From lies of tongue and pen,
> From all the easy speeches,
> That comfort cruel men,
> From sale and profanation
> Of Honour and the Sword,
> From Sleep and from Damnation
> Deliver us, Good Lord.

So freedom means responsibility; duty comes first; the rights, the privileges and the advantages derive from this source. This duty, like Winifred Maxwell's wide charity, has begun at home; no one has called and gone away without help – and a cup of tea! Beyond the home has lain her study, the libraries, the archives, the Council Chamber, the University, her fellow men and women. For her the individual's duty must expand and escalate; he or she must 'go through all the gates' to the uplands of wisdom and academic achievement; Athene does not, in real life, spring full-grown from the head of Zeus. The 'local' beginning must be firm, a base of independent opinion and Liberty's guarantee against Tyranny. Thus Professor Maxwell has frequently taken pains to emphasize that sound local government is one of the greatest props of a solid democratic state. For this second reason – the relevance of the *root* from which 'the pith of the matter' grows – we, as editors, hope that 'Local History' will prove an appropriate choice, in her eyes, for this *Festschrift*.

'Local History', which was at one time considered simply a branch of antiquarianism, is now well established as a specialized discipline. Impelled by the *Annales* School of French historians, by British scholars such as Sydney and Beatrice Webb, and more recently by the researchers at Leicester, to mention but a few, the new discipline has acquired a recognized academic status. Its concern is the concentrated study, in time-depth, of the rich variety of archaeological, written, statistical, and other source material that can be exhaustively tapped if the region investigated is small. Indeed, the sophisticated scale on which local history can be attempted is best exemplified by the magnificent, if incomplete, *Victoria County Histories of England*.

The environment studied by the local historian may vary in size – 'a village or a few villages, a small or middle-sized town . . . or a geographical area not greater than a common provincial unit' (Pierre Goubert); but whatever its size, it has an identity of its own, worth studying in its own right. Beyond this, the locality studied can provide a microscopic counterweight to the self-governing state of which it forms part: it will often emphasize and illuminate the issues that arise at the national level.

The contributions of the graduates of the Rhodes University History Department to this book vary in the depth and concentration of investigation applied to specific areas. The limitations of length unavoidably imposed upon the essays, and the above average size of certain of the selected regions or the crucial nature of the articulation with greater units have largely determined this variation. Some contributions therefore closely fit the conventional definition of 'Local History'; others more loosely. Nevertheless, all the essays do reflect a concern with developments whose implications are, at some point, significantly related to the local life of a regional entity.

Geoffrey Ellis's contribution on his findings in French provincial archives conforms entirely to the traditional view of 'Local History'. So does Vic Gatrell's consideration of Victorian Manchester. But other contributions are conceived on a broader scale. For example, Deryck Schreuder's emphasis upon the British North America Act of 1867 as the model for Gladstone's Home Rule Bill of 1886 brings together the constitutional history of two member communities of the British Empire – as mediated through the imperial legislature in London. Similarly, Richard Wood's discussion of the selection of Salisbury as capital of the Central Federation raises by implication the general question of why local interests struggle so hard to determine the positioning of federal epicentres, whether they be Washington D.C., Canberra, or Pretoria. Andrew Duminy's study concentrates upon a divided interest group – the Uitlander Council – whose varying opinions about the Transvaal regime are discharged from what may be termed 'a parish pump of imperial politics'. As such, it provides a welcome variation upon the well-used theme of 'metropolis' *vis-à-vis* 'periphery'.

Nevertheless, divisions between centre and periphery should not be overdrawn. Clio wears a seamless garment; the historical analysis of almost any major development, as already mentioned, will illuminate the interdependence between centre and circumference. The link may be that between metropolis and colony, as in Schreuder's essay, or it may be that between local and central government, as shown in Bruce Murray's original analysis of the connection between local rating and Lloyd George's 'Peoples' Budget'.

Local situations may be the laboratories where more general and representative formulae of government are first evolved or tested. Rhodes's 'Bill for Africa', the Glen Grey Act of 1894, was less representative in practice than it was meant to be in principle; but Ruth Edgecombe's essay reveals how the Cape Administration applied a new empirical principle of land-holding and local government with a view to its later extension to other areas.

Finally, 'Local History' can be said to possess readability in its own right, provided the human interest is sufficiently high. In this spirit the editors offer June Williams's description of the Anglican Establishment in Barbados and Trinidad and Paul Maylam's account of thwarted ambition on the Road to the North. In the latter essay a syndicate of Grahamstown entrepreneurs, suffering from delusions of future grandeur and possessing a capacity for complicating greater schemes than their own, 'vanished into oblivion, submerged beneath the larger concerns which came to control the white scramble'.

> Née à peine, la source tombe
> Dans le grand lac, qui l'engloutit

To Winifred Maxwell these contributions are, in gratitude, respectfully dedicated.

J. A. BENYON

C. W. COOK

T. R. H. DAVENPORT

K. S. HUNT

ALSACE AND THE FRENCH NATION
1789–1871
A View from the Archives

Geoffrey Ellis

Of the many seminal ideas Professor Winifred Maxwell has left with generations of her pupils, few have struck me more than her distinction between 'thinking points' and 'feeling points' in history. I recall her making it in the explanation of several particularly sensitive episodes in South African history. Appropriately so, yet no doubt her distinction applies to all historical issues on which writers are passionately divided. It is especially significant for local historians, who so often seem the touchiest of all. At any rate it has come back to me time and again in my work on Alsatian history. All the essential elements of an international tug of war for political and cultural identity are present in the polemical debate between the French patriots of that province ('les vrais Alsaciens' or 'die echten Elsässer') and the Pangermanists of the last century. The nerve-centre of the dispute, as far as it concerns the 19th century at least, is one's view of the German conquest and annexation of Alsace-Lorraine in 1870–1. Are we to regard this troubled episode as the 'rape' of two provinces already fully assimilated into the French nation, or as their 'reincorporation' into an older Teutonic fatherland (a most unfashionable position to take nowadays), or simply as another trauma of a Both Man's Land which the old Lotharingian ideal had failed to sustain in material form?

Posed in this way, tendentiously and provocatively, the question is not easy for an outsider to answer. When the polemicists' dispute is carried back, as it so often is, to earlier periods of Alsatian history, our vision is easily distorted. A kind of historical prolepsis tenses up the earlier 19th century with an anticipation of what is to happen in 1870–1. Whether we move backward or forward from that watershed, its world seems too much with us. There have been, not surprisingly, many conflicting French and German accounts of 1870–1. There were also at the time, and for several decades afterwards, 'official' views as seen from Paris and Berlin. For good measure, as if the polemicists' storm was not already turbulent enough, Alsatian historians have themselves written profusely in both French and German (since 1918, admittedly, mostly in French) about the meaning of that crisis.

Indeed, the first real inkling I had that something much more complex than a Franco-German conflict was at issue came when I looked at the debate from Alsace itself. The local archival records of the Strasbourgeois, Colmariens, and Mulhousiens somehow did not quite fit the 'national' views and 'official' arrogations of Alsatian allegiance emanating from Paris and Berlin. It is true that the shocking experience of 1870–1 tended to sharpen most Alsatians' awareness of their acquired 'Frenchness' and of the great wrench they had suffered. This was even in a sense an emotional compensation for the physical loss of things Alsatian. The 'feeling-points' during and after the events of 1870–1 were ready to hand. I have tried not to cultivate them, but no doubt they have filtered through by osmotic influence from the French sources and move me in a vicarious way.

What, then, of the 'thinking-points'? Perhaps one's first answer is that, ideally, earlier periods of Alsatian history *ought* not to start from a position preconditioned by 1870–1. Yet Alsatian sources for the 18th and early 19th centuries abound in material touching on the political affiliations of local communities, their cultural sympathies, religious orientation, and even their ethnic identities. The linguistic frontiers, for instance, did not square with the political ones. French and *Hochdeutsch* were the languages of the educated bourgeois (administrators, professional men and scholars) and of their schools, though not all were by any means fully articulate in both or even either. Until well into the 19th century the French officials were shocked by the number of Alsatian mayors whose spoken French was rudimentary and who could not write it at all. The mass of the population knew only some variety or other of *Elsässisch*, the local German dialect. If they were literate (and many were not), they wrote it as they spoke it, in a simple phonetic way.

French historians have often claimed, however, that the period 1789–1815 was the crucial stage in the 'Gallicization' of the Alsatian people. The word which contemporaries used was in fact *francisation*, or sometimes more provocatively *dégermanisation*. The French Revolution, with its new concept of 'Fatherland' (*Patrie*) and quasi-ideological battles, is supposed to have been the main agent in that process. After all, it was the Revolution that drove out the foreign landowners (the *princes possessionnés d'Alsace*), abolished their lay and ecclesiastical *seigneuries*, and freed the local peasantry from their oppressive feudal dues. What it profoundly changed, so the argument continues, Napoleon consolidated. In other words, Alsace was more recognizably a 'French' province in 1815 than it had been in 1789, even though German was still the predominant language of the schools and long remained so. *A fortiori*, another half-century or more of French rule during the Bourbon Restoration, the July Monarchy, the Second Republic, and the Second Empire – their concepts of 'Fatherland' make rather strange bedfellows – must surely have finished the job. 'Do you know what has made Alsace French?' Fustel de Coulanges asked in 1870, and then averred:

> Not Louis XIV, but our Revolution of 1789. Since that time Alsace has followed all our destinies; she has lived from our life. Everything we thought, she thought; everything we felt, she felt. She has shared our victories and our reverses, our glory and our mistakes, all our joys and all our sadnesses.

Had she, though? Certainly, the position of Alsace in 1789 had been anomalous. The province had been ceded to France in 1648, yet many of its largest towns had kept a measure of independence for varying periods afterwards. Strasbourg, hitherto a free imperial city, had become the provincial capital and was much the biggest urban centre when annexed by Louis XIV in 1681. The Alsatian *Décapole*, however, the ten towns[1] whose traditional affiliation was to the Holy Roman Empire, still had somewhat tenuous constitutional links with France by 1789. Mulhouse furthermore held on to its status as an independent city republic loosely associated with the Swiss cantons right up to 1798. Its citizens wished to keep it so, and only the severities of the French commercial blockade in 1796–7 forced them into a treaty of political 'reunion' with the First Republic. But at least the Mulhousiens, whose major economic interest lay in the cotton industry and more particularly in calico printing, had a material gain to show for their sacrifice. They won the freedom of the large home market in France, which under Napoleon was expanded to some 44 million subjects. The *Décapole* gained much less economically from its incorporation with revolutionary France and took rather longer to warm to its new rulers.

During the eighty-odd years before 1870–1 the formal political identity of the Alsatians remained the same, but there were some uncertain episodes. For a time in 1791–3 the counter-revolution in

Alsace, taking course and strength from the opposition of refractory priests to the Civil Constitution of the Clergy, threatened to carry the province out of the French Republic. The excesses of the Jacobin terrorists, who tended to equate provincial hostility to the authority of Paris with the crime of treason (*lèse-nation*), had a negative impact on most Alsatians. The 'Fatherland' of the 'one and indivisible Republic' drew little natural sympathy from them. The periodic visitations of army commissioners and Jacobin strongmen, regarded as 'aliens' or *parachutistes* from the interior, were also counter-productive. They did not silence the refractory clergy, who enjoyed shelter and support from the rural population, and they provoked at least one mass-flight of labourers across the Rhine. One may well, ask how *francisés* the 25 000 or 30 000 terrified innocents of the 'Grande Fuite' or 'Massenflucht' of December 1793 can have been.

On the other hand, the French military advances of 1794 brought command of the 'natural frontier' along the Rhine and ensured that Alsace would not pass to the Austrians and their allies. In due course the province became the base of the fifth Imperial military division and a focal point for the movement of troops and transports in the east. The populous class of professional *militaires* in Alsace had good reason to be loyal to the Republic and, after it, to Napoleon. Another major crisis had to be averted however at the Vienna peace negotiations of 1814–15. Some of the envoys would have liked to rub in the punishment of France by detaching Alsace and reinstating the former *princes possessionés* or their heirs. Certain lands with a total of between 60 000 and 65 000 inhabitants were in fact removed; but in the end the province and its population of around 800 000 passed in substantial part to the restored Bourbon monarchy. From then until the Franco-Prussian war the Alsatians experienced all the essential struggles and changes of French politics, though with significant nuances and variations attributable to their distance from Paris. They had their 'Ultras', moderate royalists, and out-on-a-wing liberals during the Restoration; their constitutional monarchists and liberal reformers under Louis-Philippe; their 'Reds' and 'Bonapartists' during the Second Republic, which began as a contest broadly between town and country. With the huge popular vote for Louis-Napoleon in the plebiscite of 1852, the Alsatians like other provincial peoples settled down under the Second Empire to a new experiment in the 'politics of assimilation'.

The calm was deceptive. The German bombardment of Strasbourg in August 1870 destroyed far more than the old prefecture and historic *Douane*, symbols of the French administrative and commercial traditions. Its damage to the cathedral and razing of the palace of justice struck eyewitnesses as a fearful portent of what might be expected from their conquerors. Much in the libraries and archives, the written record of Alsatian 'Frenchness', was also obliterated. Yet the Germans were well aware that they could not easily uproot those French institutions. When in 1872 the first stones of a new German university were laid in Strasbourg, purportedly 'to cultivate the sciences in the service of truth', their attempt was under way to create an academic tradition in Alsace alongside their new administrative and archival systems. In 1884 that foundation was renamed 'the University of Kaiser Wilhelm' and invested with the much more pointed official aim of propagating 'German science and the German spirit'. Here again, then, in a retrospective and oblique way, we appear to have evidence of how far the 'Frenchness' of the Alsatians had extended by 1871 and of how perversely unassimilable they seemed to their conquerors at the start of the German 'occupation' of 1871–1914.

*   *   *

Now, if I have sometimes wondered whether that much-asserted 'French' face of the Alsatians before 1870–1 is not in some ways an overdrawn mask, it is not because I wanted to think any less well of them than the French patriots of 1871–1914 did. It is only that I have always been struck more by the regional patriotism of the Alsatians than by their simulated joy in other, larger, grander causes across the Vosges. In this respect the harsh quirks of history have forced the Alsatians to acquire the qualities of the seasoned chameleon. If their 'Frenchness' in 1870–1 ran deep, as we are assured it did, we had better be clear about what sort of 'Frenchness' it really was.

For a start, the Alsatian reaction to rule from Paris had been far from always benign during the period 1789–1871. 'The dictatorship of Paris', that old battle-cry of political militants in provincial France, did not begin with the counter-revolution of 1793. It had had a voice in Bourbon France, as Alexis de Tocqueville later observed, and it has had echoes in Alsace ever since. Nor, conversely, was the Parisian view of the loyalty and peaceableness of the Alsatians always sweet. For instance, in the Year II the Committee of Public Safety reported in cruder vein that 'the provinces are peopled with egoists'. Its many political successors in Paris often had occasion to look upon Alsatian subjects as unruly frontiersmen obsessed with their own worries, and sometimes even as a 'race apart'. At any rate, one constant base survived at the centre of the see-saw battle for the 'national' allegiance of the Alsatians. This was their sharp sense of *regional* loyalty, and it was liable to break down into fairly small units of local identification, especially in times of stress.

To talk of the provincial patriotism of the Alsatians is, then, itself, an oversimplification. To be more accurate, one needs to think in terms of a mass of local particularisms which were often at loggerheads. The archival records offer only a fractional insight, usually once removed by courtesy of administrative or police reports, into the moods and behaviour of local communities. The solidarity of such particular affiliations in times before the advent of the mass media saw the Alsatians through many scrapes and crises. It was the outgrowth of restricted village life, of the demands of the agricultural cycle, of poor communications and a fragmentary market structure in most parts, of a simply educated peasantry and urban working class. Its charity began at home; there, too, it ended.

More significantly, perhaps, the same local patriotism was evident among Alsatian 'notables', notwithstanding a certain cosmopolitan fellowship common to influential frontiersmen. There is a continuous thread here between the Alsatian *cahiers de doléances* of 1789, which all commentators agree reveal a regional particularism second to none in France, and the countless petitions for redress of local grievances up to the end of the Second Empire. The specific issues of protest changed with the times, of course, but the local clamour for more generous consideration of Alsatian interests remained familiarly the same. Even the language of complaint, borrowing from an archetypical phraseology of woe, had the same repetitive ring, which may explain the administrative deafness with which it was usually met in Paris. The Alsatian *cahiers* of 1789, for instance, reveal many divergent pulls and sectional interests, but the plea for the preservation of the historic rights and privileges of the Alsatians *vis-à-vis* the central government was common to them. All the Alsatian estates wanted a larger say in local government through regional institutions, both lay and clerical. Their demands were aimed at much more than the devolution of administrative chores. They sought the decentralization of real political authority, such as the right to determine the composition of local assemblies and to decide on local taxes. The Constituent Assembly, however, thought differently. Alsace (the Bas-Rhin and Haut-Rhin) was brought into the national administrative structure of the 83 departments and their subdivisions into regular districts, cantons, and communes by the reforms of 1789–90.

The same sense of local interests infused the Alsatian *cahiers* on economic questions. All the petitions supported the special economic relationship Alsace had enjoyed under the old regime as a so-called *province à l'instar de l'étranger effectif*. The request was that the province should remain independent of the *cinq grosses fermes*, the central customs area which Colbert had established over most of the kingdom. The specific pressure-point here was the 'barriers', the cordon of local tolls stretching along the Vosges and Rhine as a visible sign of Alsatian customs independence. In spite of repeated pleas for their preservation and for the province to remain 'effectively foreign' for customs purposes, the Assembly abolished the 'barriers' in 1790 as part of its attack on internal obstacles to trade. Alsace was assimilated into the national customs system, a prolific source of grievances for many decades afterwards. Local 'notables', the chief beneficiaries of the old 'barriers' and always their own worst prophets of doom, predicted the ruin of Alsatian trade. In fact, however, the results of the repeal were more salutary than otherwise. While a few privileged individuals or corporations lost their exclusive toll dues without compensation, the merchant class as a whole benefited from the opening up of the Vosges as something like a commercial freeway from Paris and the south of France to Strasbourg and so on to the Rhenish *hinterland*.

Whatever the Revolution's very mixed political reception and economic effects in Alsace, it did open up closer communications between the province and the French interior. Ironically, the same process of assimilation with France that was to be the moral basis of the 'rape' argument in 1871 evinced a quite different response from Alsatians at the beginning of our period. It is clear, too, that if the impact of the Revolution in this process was brutal, it was also in the end effective. By the time Napoleon established the prefectorial system in France early in 1800, Alsace was no longer the maverick fringe of French influence it had once been. Nor was it any longer an economic half-way station sandwiched between two powers which played tug-of-war for its formal allegiance. The Alsatians may still have viewed their fortunes more in relation to their foreign neighbours beyond the Rhine than to their fellow countrymen across the Vosges; but politically, administratively, militarily, and to a certain extent economically they had been brought inside the French national system. The process was widely extended through the various Napoleonic codes – civil, commercial, criminal and penal – whose influence of course long survived their creators.

*   *   *

These delayed effects of the revolutionary reforms apparently did not satisfy the wishes of all Alsatians. Nor did their closer incorporation with the vast and polyglot Napoleonic Empire weaken their local patriotism. Contrary to the old textbook notion that provincial public opinion under Napoleon was simply an 'appalling nothingness' (*riennisme affreux*), archival records show that the regional life of the Empire was diverse rather than uniform. Moreover, local opinions were by no means always muted. The Alsatians at least showed remarkable temerity at times in their communications with the central government. Right up to 1815, and beyond, the ministries in Paris were subjected to a barrage of protests and petitions for redress. Sometimes the grievance was that the law of 28 April 1803, the basis of Strasbourg's trading system, allowed merchants too few rights in the entrepôt and transit traffic of the Rhine valley. Sometimes it was that the customs severities of the Continental Blockade disrupted commercial dealings with foreign states. Often the problem concerned technical difficulties in working the Rhine shipping zones. Two specific issues, the State tobacco monopoly of 1810 and the closure of Strasbourg to Levantine cotton imports in 1812, were bitterly resented by interested parties, whose instinct was not to suffer in silence.

The Alsatians developed many rhetorical ploys to back their protests. Exaggeration for effect, ironic contrast with a presumed prosperity across the Rhine, the special needs of frontier people, golden age conceits, and so on: these were the preferred hobby-horses to bear the weight of local grievances. The golden age conceit was particularly intrusive. It nostalgically invoked an era of magnificent prosperity before the revolutionary blight. With the passage of time this myth was embellished by all sorts of fabulous tales of a former Alsatian commonwealth withered away to dust and ashes. It was as if the cycle of fat and lean kine had got stuck in its thin phase, as if an economic ice age had gripped the province. Too many historians have taken this sort of overdone rhetoric at face value.

In reality, however, the Alsatians on the whole did not fare badly under Napoleonic rule. There was first the seasonal luck of good harvests, with an exceptionally good cycle in 1806-9, and no real trouble emerged on this front until the brief panic in 1812. Plentiful grain stocks for most of the Empire precluded what otherwise would have been the normal inflationary effect of a prolonged war on food prices. Secondly, between 1800 and 1806 merchants and manufacturers alike recovered from their revolutionary losses. In the years 1807-10, when the Continental System and the British naval blockade of the Continental coastline turned French trade inland towards the mainland markets, the Strasbourgeois benefited more than most from such deflected traffic. The city then lay at the hub of the reorientated traffic lanes used under the Blockade's regime. It became, as contemporaries liked to say, 'le boulevard de la France'. I estimate from official statistics (which tell us nothing about the enormously lucrative smuggling trade) that its entrepôt and transit traffic increased by at least 50% compared with the period before the Blockade. It handled as much as a third of all imperial imports. As for the Alsatian industries, production in Mulhouse and most other manufacturing towns of the Haut-Rhin was boosted by higher demand on the home market and favourable opportunities for export. The economic crisis of 1810-11 hit Alsace, as it did most of western Europe, but did not destroy the progress of the earlier years. What followed to the end of the Empire was slow and hard-won recovery.

Yet strangely one finds little or only grudging admission in contemporary Alsatian documents that Napoleonic rule had a positive side. 'Bonapartism' and its accompanying belief that all had been well under the great emperor were later developments. They battened on the political instability of the restored Bourbons and on Louis-Philippe's immobility in reform. They were also helped by the economic troubles of 1825-30 and 1846-51. In perhaps the most illuminating single set of Alsatian documents with which I have worked, one has a generally bleak view of local reaction to the policies of the central government. I refer to the stout minute-books of the chamber of commerce in Strasbourg, which are continuous and immaculately kept from its foundation in March 1803 until the German conquest. Composed of, or at least representing, the commercial and financial magnates, this body was the natural forum for discussion of local grievances. It usually sent its protests and petitions to the prefects in the first instance, and these officials on the whole supported them in their correspondence with Paris. Lezay-Marnésia, prefect in 1810–14 and one with the reputation of being 'fou pour le bien',* was formally rebuked on more than one occasion by the minister Montalivet for taking the side of Alsatian dissidents in their various quarrels with the government.

The chamber's minute-books for the first half of the 19th century clearly illustrate the frontier complex ingrained in most Alsatians. Believing that their situation was unique, they made the simple inference that they ought to be allowed special prerogatives in the Rhenish frontier trade. Long after the Continental System had collapsed; after the allied invasions of 1814–15 and the weather-cock-like welcoming addresses of the two Bourbon restorations and Hundred Days had passed; after the economic crisis of 1816–17 had eased and the Württemberg contingent of the allied army of occupation had left Alsace in a stink, the chamber still apparently had cause for almost incessant protest. At the highest level such disaffection was communicated discreetly through Alsatian deputies like Humann and Turckheim and (in the Haut-Rhin) Koechlin. At the popular level groups which were 'agin the government' (and often any government would do) met in coffee-houses to vent their spleen, or read the mounting criticism of the Parisian authorities in the *Courrier du Bas-Rhin*. It was as if this local cantankerousness, the legendary 'esprit frondeur des Alsaciens', was the *quid pro quo* for their ultimate acquiescence in the political regimes of the Restoration and July Monarchy. They made the central government work hard, if only administratively, for their grudging support. Nothing much changed here until the peasant franchise of 1848 opened the way to huge and demonstrable popular majorities.

If it was not the restrictions placed on the Alsatian tobacco trade that offended the chamber in Strasbourg, it was the inadequacy of the city's entrepôt status, or the dispute between merchants and manufacturers over the protectionist tariffs. In the 1820s the Strasbourgeois wanted the rights of a 'free port' for their city, but this was refused many times. The Rhine shipping convention of 1831,

---

*This popular phrase of the time defies accurate translation, but its idiom may be captured by some such wording as 'crazy about doing good'.

which finally 'freed' navigation to all riverain communities, upset the long-established bargees. In the 1840s the government's slow and reluctant encroachment into the area of industrial supervision irked the cotton entrepreneurs and the iron-masters of the Haut-Rhin. *Laissez-faire* seemed to them a natural alternative more consonant with the sense of honour of their Protestant *fabricantocratie*. The government's railway policy in the 1850s, which sucked capital out of the province for investment in distant projects, was not welcomed by the Alsatian houses which depended on local credit. Yet perhaps the most recurrent theme after 1815 was the economic rivalry within Alsace between the merchant interests of Strasbourg and the industrial lobby in Mulhouse. The chamber thought that the first had been sacrificed to the second, and to be fair their objective performances rather underlined the point. While the river trade of Strasbourg after 1815 entered an eclipse lasting several decades, partly because the old maritime routes had revived, the industries of Mulhouse expanded impressively. Whereas the population of Mulhouse trebled to 18 000 between 1798 and 1830, that of Strasbourg was lower at the latter date than its level of over 50 000 in 1814. The completion of the Rhône-Rhine canal benefited the Haut-Rhin, through which it ran, more than its neighbouring department. It was not for nothing that Mulhouse was then known as 'le Manchester français'.

The protests and petitions of the Strasbourgeois recurred so frequently that they sound like orchestrated variations on the theme of doomsday. They vary in pitch from the injured innocence of reason unrequited to the darkest pessimism of despair. But the reader soon learns that the chamber was indulging in a kind of negative public relations exercise. In doing so it drove its protests to the point of 'over-kill'. The central government was concerned to apply national policies as uniformly as possible, and in any case it was weighed down with similar material from all over France. It seemed to the Alsatians to be caught up in aggregations and remote bureaucratic processes. This view through the archival 'telescope' is much the same whether one takes it from the chamber's meeting rooms at Place Gutenberg or from the much fuller departmental archives of the Bas-Rhin in Rue Fishart. If however one reverses the telescope and looks at Alsace from the Parisian end, from say the central repository of the Archives Nationales, the vista is quite different. Instead of a tense bunch of urgent local problems one finds more filtered evidence of a distant disgruntlement, an irritating frontier murmuring, a dull but persistent belly-ache at the far end of one administrative pipeline among many. Receipt of repeated protests and petitions for redress was all part of the dreary everyday work occupying the ministries in Paris. Not surprisingly, they grew a thick skin in their handling of such business.

*   *   *

If one may conclude that by 1871 Alsace had been assimilated into the French nation in many material ways, it had never been (in the French sense) 'spiritually annexed'. Its people maintained their sense of local independence and often squinted in the face of 'national' decisions. More Alsatians spoke French as their mother tongue than in 1789, and many more could speak it in a fashion, thanks to a longer and closer familiarity with French administrative habits. If more Frenchmen from the interior were ready to settle in Alsace by the end of our period, rather than regard it as a grim stepping-stone to a grander career elsewhere, only a few Alsatian prefects before 1871 were in fact natives of the province. Access to an *école normale* had been possible in the Bas-Rhin since 1811 and in the other Alsatian department since 1833; yet German was not only allowed in such schools but still predominated in the province at large. Witnesses record that German was even then the usual language for sermons and other church activities. As for the religious communities, Roman Catholic and Protestant had learnt to coexist, though bitter memories of the 1790s and of Charles X's spiritual neuroses lay not far from the surface. The Jews had come to enjoy that status not unfamiliar to them of notional legal equality matched by actual social disabilities.

Altogether, Alsace on the eve of the German conquest was socially much less of a patchwork and isolated part of France than when the Revolution had caught it unawares. Better roads and in due course the railways and Rhine steamships had opened it up to visitors and traffic in a way that would probably have appalled the proud frontiers-men of 1789. It had become, in short, a more populous and economic-ally more important French province, which was not the least reason for Bismarck's interest in it. But its spokesmen remained true to form in their preoccupation with local problems and the special needs, as they saw them, of frontier communities. The horrors of 1870–1 did more in a few months than the central government in some eighty years to make the Alsatians feel 'French' to the marrow. But on the eve of the conquest they were Alsatians first and Frenchmen second. If this particular experience can be accommodated in Professor Maxwell's generous understanding of local history, as I trust it can, then the Alsatians are not out of place in a volume such as this.

NOTE ON SOURCES

Many of the primary sources for Alsatian history from the Revolution to the German conquest were destroyed during the bombardment of 1870, but the surviving official records remain vast. They are available in three major repositories: the Archives Nationales (Paris), and the departmental archives of the Bas-Rhin (Strasbourg) and Haut-Rhin (Colmar). My 'view from the archives' is based, in the first case, on cartons in the central sub-series F^1 (General Administration), F^2 (Departmental Administration), F^7 (Police), F^{12} (Trade and Industry), and AF^{IV} (State Secretariat – Napoleonic period).

At provincial level this essay draws primarily on the sub-series XII M and XIII M in Strasbourg and I M in Colmar. The series R in Strasbourg (military papers) and P in Colmar (customs and smuggling) have also been useful. Of the municipal archives, those at Strasbourg (series B3) and Colmar (series REC to REH) are much more detailed than the somewhat disappointing material in Mulhouse (series F^{II} to F^{VIII}).

Easily the principal source for the economic history of Strasbourg, and the origin of most prefectoral reports on the city and on the Bas-Rhin more generally, is the set of minute-books of the Chamber of Commerce and Industry at Place Gutenberg. Starting with the Chamber's foundation in 1803, and kept in immense detail, these are more or less complete for my period. Most of the other records of the Chamber were transferred to the departmental archives in Rue Fishart in 1964.

Of the mass of printed secondary sources available, special mention must be made of the publications of the Société Savante d'Alsace et des Régions de l'Est: notably the volumes *Deux siècles d'Alsace francaise: 1648, 1798, 1848* (ed. F. Ponteil, 1948), *La bourgeoisie alsacienne* (ed. J. Schlumberger, 1954), *Paysans d'Alsace* (ed. R. Redslob, 1959), and *Artisans et ouvriers d'Alsace* (ed. H. Haug, 1965). Valuable material has also been published in the *Bulletin de la Société Industrielle de Mulhouse* (from 1836), in the *Revue d'Alsace* (Colmar, from 1850), and in the *Zeitscrift für die Geschichte des Oberrheins* (Karlsruhe, from 1850).

---

1. Colmar, Haguenau, Landau, Munster, Kaysersberg, Oberehenheim, Rosheim, Sélestat, Turckheim, and Wissembourg.

A MANCHESTER PARABLE

V. A. C. Gatrell

The chimney of the world! Rich rascals, poor rogues, drunken ragamuffins and prostitutes, form the moral; soot made into paste form the physique; and the only view is a long chimney: what a place! The entrance to hell realized!

—GENERAL NAPIER, 1839

Early 19th century Manchester has appropriately if inelegantly been termed the 'shock city' of its age: a place as full of omen in that period as London was towards the end of the century or Tokyo or New York may be for us today. An apocalyptic note sounds through the writings of those who visited the town in the 1830s and 1840s – and there were many such visitors, grimly parodying the Grand Tour of a more innocent age. If Disraeli could proclaim Manchester a new Athens, de Tocqueville, like Napier (and more plausibly), found in its grimy streets a new Hades. There, wrote another observer, was gathered 'an aggregate of masses, our conceptions of which clothe themselves in terms that express something portentous and fearful'. In Manchester mighty forces for change were at work, to be compared with 'the slow rising and gradual swelling of an ocean which must, at some future and no distant time, bear all the elements of society aloft upon its bosom, and float them – Heaven knows whither'.[1]

It was not so much the size of the place that accounted for these overblown hyperboles, nor even its slums or its factories. Manchester had grown explosively, but even in the 1840s you could walk across the town in half an hour and never be far from the distant prospect of hills and fields, even if they were ravaged by canals and dye-works. Its squalor could be matched in Birmingham, Leeds and London itself. And its giant factories were in fact few; most were merely rather large workshops. The real significance of the place, as contemporaries saw it, lay in the awful confrontation there of class with class. 'At Manchester', de Tocqueville wrote, 'a few great capitalists, thousands of poor workmen'. 'There is nothing', wrote another French visitor, 'but masters and operatives'. 'There is no town in the world', a local cleric asserted, 'where the distance between the

28

rich and the poor is so great, or the barrier between them is so difficult to be crossed'.[2] Assertions of this kinds have impressed later generations with the belief that had England experienced a revolution, it would most likely have originated here; and certainly the cathartic experiences of the Peterloo massacre in 1819, the reform riots of 1831–2, and the plug-drawing riots of 1842, give some weight to that belief.

For all that, any historian who examines the town's history closely must be struck by a curious paradox. The depth of social cleavage in Manchester is not to be contested; nor are the chronic intensity of working class resentment and the harsh realities of economic and social inequality. The remarkable fact remains that, throughout these decades, it was very seldom that propertied men there were as directly affected by, or even as conscious of, the antagonisms of those who laboured for them as those conditions might lead us to expect. With very few exceptions, the apocalypse was being anticipated by outsiders, not by middle class Mancunians themselves. So it was, for example, that while the rest of the world trembled for the conflicts to come, a local merchant could observe in 1833 that there was 'always a little commotion in Manchester, but not very material'. While Peel agonized about the structural causes of distress in the early 1840s, the editor of the *Manchester Courier* could weakly resign himself to the fact that 'periodical distress is inseparable from the vicissitudes of trade', and leave it at that.

While James Kay rebuked those who attributed 'popular tumults . . . (merely) to the instigation of unprincipled leaders, – as though a happy people could love discord', the local Chamber of Commerce could blandly ascribe the plug riots (no minor disturbance, but one which exposed the bitterness and desperation of skilled artisans as well as casual labourers, of English engineers as well as Irish navvies) to chartist demagogues' 'efforts to mislead the operatives of this district'. Even in the wake of that upheaval, there were those who could persuade themselves that popular grievances could 'at once and forever' be dispelled by 'a few kind words from any respected superior'.[3] Was this seeming myopia on the part of Manchester's respectable inhabitants born simply of a more intimate knowledge of the town – a sense, perhaps, that outsiders were ignorant of the intrinsic stability of the place, or that they were wilfully alarmist? Or was it born of a form of culpable blindness, a deliberate refusal to admit the realities of their position in an acutely exploitative and segregated society?

Doubtless these muted responses to suffering did reflect in part an informed confidence in the security of local authority which the town's visitors lacked. Mancunians might be aware, for example, that this was not in fact a 'pure' cotton town such as Oldham or Bolton, in which masters and men faced each other almost alone. It was a provincial retailing and servicing capital as well as a manufacturing centre, in which artisans and craftsmen outnumbered factory workers and shopkeepers outnumbered 'capitalists'. So the *Courier's* editor could plausibly speak of the 'harmlessness' of popular radicalism in Manchester, aware as he was of 'the utter impossibility of reconciling the conflicting interests' within an immensely heterogeneous population. Nor should we discount the confidence generated by the sheer physical power at the authorities' disposal – a body of police consolidated by the town's incorporation in 1838; the presence in 1842 of up to 2 000 soldiers in local barracks; a force of special constables which at its peak in August 1842 – as the plug riots raged – numbered over 6 000; and an efficient spy system which infiltrated private as well as public chartist meetings. Local chartism was laid low by this machinery. Allowing for the unrecorded numbers discharged with a caution or against whom proceedings were dropped, it is probable that near on a thousand people were arrested for political or near-political offences in the Manchester area in the chartist decade as a whole. The policy of mass arrest was the buttress upon which, in critical months, the survival of Manchester society depended. If it had failed, of course, there was always the ultimate sanction of the military. 'Poor people. They will suffer', General Napier wrote as he took up the command of the troops in the northern district in 1839:

> They have set all England against them and their physical force: fools! We have the physical force, not they. They talk of their hundreds of thousands of men. Who is to move them when I am dancing around them with cavalry, and pelting them with cannon-shot? What would their hundred thousand men do with my hundred rockets wriggling their fiery tails among them, roaring, scorching, tearing, smashing all they come near? . . . Poor men! Poor men! How little they know of physical force.[4]

Considerations such as these (and, one might add, the long-term conditioning of influential sections of the workforce into a respect for property and the constitution, as well as the acute competition for employment which weakened Manchester trade unionism) go some way to account for respectable people's confidence in the stability both of their own society and of the nation at large. But there is more to our problem than that. The historian is confronted in the Manchester middle class, in extreme form, with a cast of mind which was enclosed and inward-turning, self-referential and self-protective. These appear to be people whose ease of mind about the privileges they enjoyed in that town was purchased at high cost – by a narrowing of the imagination and sympathies.

In respect of some of their attitudes, of course, Mancunians were no more culpable than the rest of their fellow-countrymen. One notes, for example, an inclination there as elsewhere to regard 'politics' as something to do primarily with the allocation of authority within the privileged group, or with the advancement of that group's interest in the nation at large. How could it be otherwise when the electoral system confined the vote to under a fifth of adult males in the town? There were, however, some distinctive characteristics about the Manchester electorate which further narrowed the mental horizons of local politicians. An electorate of between ten and twelve thousand was too large, for example, for the non-electorate to exercise that influence by boycott which was possible in smaller industrial boroughs; it was too large, also, for the rank-and-file to have a chance of organizing it. (And this would have had interesting possibilities, for just under a half of all voters were artisans or shopkeepers.) It could be manipulated only by a caucus system which threw local influence unambiguously into the hands of well-heeled and committee élites. The result was that 'official' Manchester politics had little to do with factory reform, or with poor law or police control, as was the case in neighbouring Oldham, for example. Politics instead had everything to do with the preoccupations of men of property and business: the contest for local authority between a tory and high church group and its 'liberal' and (loosely) nonconformist challengers; and above all the issue of the corn laws and foreign markets, which the Cobdenite caucus brought to the hustings with well-known results. The consequence was that while some third of the 'popular' electorate regularly abstained from the exercise of their votes, the animosities generated by these issues among the wealthy few were intense: for such men, they comprised the stuff of politics. And what is important in the present context is that they had virtually no reference to the battle which so impressed outsiders, that which was alleged to exist between capital and labour. Indeed, the inward-looking nature of the middle class political consciousness at this level, and its blindness to what may nowadays strike us as the more critical confrontations within Manchester society, are neatly encapsulated in the comment of that Midland tory who felt that 'the Chartists . . . are a much more jolly straightforward set of fellows than the Whigs'.[5]

Even if much of this must be taken for granted, we are still left with our central conundrum. Except in unusually prosperous years, the extent of mass impoverishment and bitterness in Manchester was self-evident: 'There is among the manufacturing poor a stern look of discontent, a hatred of all who are rich, a total absence of merry faces'. Napier wrote: 'a sallow tinge and dirty skins tell of suffering and brooding over change'. If outsiders could see this, why could the Manchester rich not, even allowing for their political isolation? Or if they did see it, why did they resign themselves to it with such apparent ease as the necessary price of their own comfort?

The answer is a familiar one. It lay in the use they could make of a doctrine which neatly validated self-interest. By the 1830s the popular assault on the rights of property had effectively driven the middle classes into one camp – not least in a town where new wealth, and new property, were being created at a rate unprecedented in human history. The consequence was that despite their internal squabbles they shared a remarkable homogeneous intellectual culture whose assumptions were not seriously to be questioned until the 1850s. They were, in short, under the spell of some popularized version of Ricardian political economy, and their sensitivities were anaesthetized by it.

Dickens' portrayal of Messrs Gradgrind and Bounderby illustrates how well this point was taken by the metropolitan culture. To find caricature embodied in real flesh and blood can be startling, but the experience is not an uncommon one for the Manchester historian. Take, for example, the justification of the subsistence wage advanced by W. R. Greg, Anti-Corn Law Leaguer and member of one of the greatest northern cotton families. His writings in the *Edinburgh Review* are grim classics of their kind, but a few quotations will here suffice to convey their flavour:[6]

The first duty which the great employer of labour owes to those who work for him is to make his business succeed . . . This . . . imposes upon the employer the duty of not allowing any benevolent plans or sentiments of lax kindness to interfere with the main purpose in view . . . He must not scruple to reduce wages where the well-being of the undertaking renders this change indispensable.

Such scruples in any case, Greg believed, would be pointless: wages would find their own level as by a law of nature:

Neither the most boundless benevolence, nor the most consummate ability, can fight against the clear moral and material laws of the universe. If the field of employment is too limited for the numbers who crowd into it, no power and no goodness can prevent wages from falling.

On this view of things it went without saying that

We cannot raise the mass out of their misery – they must raise themselves. State interference is omnipotent for evil – very impotent for good . . . The State . . . must act upon principles as stern, as steady, and as comprehensive as those of Nature herself.

To assume that it could be otherwise was to exhibit that

unsound, exaggerated, and somewhat maudlin tenderness with which it is now the fashion to regard the criminal and the pauper [a revealing equation] . . . This sensitive aversion to the affliction or the sight of pain is, in truth, the characteristic, and the special peril, of the practical [philanthropy] of the day.

More subtle polemicists, not to mention the political economists themselves, surrounded such assertions of the intrinsic value and 'naturalness' of the free market system with a network of qualifications and exceptions which softened their bleaker implications for the labouring poor. Not so Greg: though extracted from context, quotations of this kind do him little injustice. Nor was it surprising that his Manchester readers should have acquiesced in their wisdom; simplified political economy provided a powerful armoury for the assault on trade unionists, factory reformers, and those misguided few (outside Manchester) who babbled of state-assisted welfare.

Of course the dourness of the Manchester mind was not altogether unrelieved. Perhaps the *Manchester Guardian*, in 1854, had just cause to equate 'that ever-fresh conception of Manchester as the shop and factory of a parcel of long-headed, cold-blooded fellows, who revel in unholy wealth' with the comic stereotypes of the English milord or the English Jack Tar. In Mrs Gaskell there was at least one who sought imaginatively to come to terms with the population of the back-streets as if they were real human beings. And a few voices (of clerics and doctors mainly: not the *Guardian's*) were repeatedly raised against the conditions in which the poor lived. But too often the stranglehold of political economy rendered even their good intentions nugatory. Thus Peter Gaskell's *Artisans and Machinery* (1836) remains among the most eloquent of contemporary indictments of the factory system upon which Manchester's wealth was erected. But even Gaskell retreated from at least one of the logical conclusions implicit in his investigations – that working men should unionize – on grounds not very different from Greg's: 'Labour's value is given to it by the demand, and the (employer) . . . so calling it into demand, has . . . an obvious right to rate it as may seem . . . its fair equivalent'. Indeed, impotent as they were to propose a solution to the Manchester malaise other than that which might derive from the ever continuing expansion of the free market economy, these few honourable critics were often obliged to express their indignation in the reduction of social evils to 'statistics'. They could, and voluminously did, count the number of cellar dwellings in the Old Town, the number of cesspools to a street, the number of illegitimate births in a year: it was not for nothing that Manchester saw the establishment in 1833 of Britain's first Statistical Society, which in its early years justified itself mainly in these sombre recordings. Their tacit acquiescence was ill-conceived, of course; state intervention was to prove essential to the relief of urban conditions, and Ruskin spoke truly when in 1857 he told an understandably hostile audience at the Manchester Athenaeum that 'the "Let-alone" principle is, in all things which men have to deal with, the principle of death'. But we can understand their plight. Who in that closed community could talk of statutory wage regulation or the redistributive taxation of wealth and hope to retain his respectable standing?[7]

In a sense the plight of these people went even deeper than that. Living, as Hippolyte Taine found, in their mansions of 'equivocal and trumpery luxury' (where hosts and dinner guests 'all drink port for three hours at a stretch without saying anything'), Manchester's captains of industry themselves led bleak lives. 'Music and the fine arts generally were not practised in our circle', a diarist recalls, 'and the lighter amenities of life were unknown to us'. A seventeen-year-old destined for his father's counting-house inscribes solemnly in his commonplace-book, 'Remember that time is money . . . Remember that credit is money'. In the correspondence columns of the *Guardian* a brave young wife speaks up against the inclination of Manchester husbands to absent themselves at the mill 'until the lingering hours appear like days':

> It is to please them that our conversation is so often directed to trivial objects, and we talk nonsense because that and calicoes (of which we know nothing) are the only things they can understand or listen to with pleasure . . . If they either could or would take the trouble . . . they would find that we are not the frivolous and illiterate creatures it appears we are generally considered.

Flashes of self-recognition in this community are rare; but the great mill-owner Henry Ashworth allowed himself at least one:

> We are a peculiar class who happen to have jumped into this line of business. Active pursuits have become identified with our own enjoyments and our habits, and we have eventually raised up a heap of capital and large buildings. All our pleasures and all our hopes are completely identified with them; and but very few persons not connected with the trade would like to change places with us.[8]

For the most part, however, this was a social class cocooned from a full realization of the moral bankruptcy of their society and the penalties it was exacting from those who laboured for them. It was some decades before their self-esteem was to be pricked, and even then it was not by any confrontation mounted by working men. In 1869, in *Culture and Anarchy*, Matthew Arnold was to single out eminent Manchester spokesmen – John Bright and W. R. Greg among them – as Philistines, as men excluded from the pursuit and recognition of sweetness and light, as men isolated from the mainstream of English culture. The shock was profound. Arnold, like Ruskin a decade before him, had looked upon Disraeli's new Athens and found it – provincial! Perhaps it was only by scorn that men in their position, so well protected by the armoury of the state they despised, so arrogant in the righteousness of their calling, could be truly touched.

NOTES

1. B. Disraeli, *Coningsby* (1844); A. de Tocqueville, *Journeys to England and Ireland* (1957 ed.), p. 107; W. Cooke Taylor, *Notes of a Tour in the Manufacturing Districts of Lancashire* (1841), pp. 13, 38.

2. De Tocqueville, *op. cit.*, pp. 104–5; L. Faucher, *Manchester in 1844* (1844), p. 21; Rev. R. Parkinson, *The Present Condition of the Labouring Poor in Manchester* (1841).

3. *Parliamentary Papers*, 1833, VI Q.5166; R. Sowler, 'The League's Revenge', *Blackwood's Magazine*, LII (1842), 542–60; T. de Quincey, 'The Anti-Corn Law Deputations to Sir Robert Peel', *Blackwood's Magazine*, LII (1842), 275–6; J. P. Kay, *The Moral and Physical Condition of the Working Classes . . . in Manchester* (1832), pp. 8–9; *Minutes* of Manchester Chamber of Commerce (Manchester Library), Feb. 1843; Parkinson, *loc. cit.*

4. W. Napier, *Life and Opinions of General Sir Charles Napier* (1857), pp. 11, 57.

5. Quoted by G. Kitson Clark, 'The Electorate and the Repeal of the Corn Laws', *Transactions of the Royal Historical Society*, I (1950), p. 123.

6. W. R. Greg, 'Employers and Employed', *Edinburgh Review*, XCIII (1851), pp. 22–71, and 'Unsound Social Philosophy', *Edinburgh Review*, XC (1849), pp. 196–524.

7. *Manchester Guardian*, 20 May 1854; J. Ruskin, *A Joy for Ever (and its Price on the Market)*.

8. H. Taine, *Notes on England* (1872 ed.), p. 224; A. Neild, *Recollections* (typescript, 1898: Rylands Library); Richard Potter, *Diary* (Manuscript, L.S.E.); *Manchester Guardian*, 1 Aug. 1829; H. Ashworth in *Parliamentary Papers*, 1846, VI (i), QQ. 3934–8.

LLOYD GEORGE AND THE LAND:
The Issue of Site-Value Rating

Bruce K. Murray

It is sometimes contended that David Lloyd George's primary purpose in including land value duties in his famous 'People's Budget' of 1909–10 was to provoke the House of Lords into rejecting the Budget, and thereby precipitate the decisive confrontation between the Liberal Government and the Lords. The contention is that the 'People's Budget' was designed as a trap, into which the Lords duly fell in November 1909 when they refused to pass the Budget. After two closely contested general elections in 1910, the Lords finally paid the penalty in 1911 when they were forced to consent to the passage of the Parliament Bill, which drastically reduced the powers of the Upper House.

Evidence now available, however, reinforces the counter-argument that Lloyd George's purpose in including the land value duties in the 'People's Budget' was not to goad the peers but to circumvent the veto of the Lords on the question of land valuation. Indeed, some of the new evidence suggests that, so far from setting out to provoke the Lords into rejection by means of the land value duties, part of Lloyd George's original intention in incorporating those duties in his Budget was to warn off the peers from carrying out the threat made by some Unionists to force a general election by having the Finance Bill for 1909–10 rejected in the Lords. At any rate, until mid-July 1909 Lloyd George seems in his private conversations and correspondence to have consistently contended that the Lords would only throw out the Budget if they saw it to be unpopular, and that the land value duties were vital to ensure its popularity in the country.[1] It was after his notorious Limehouse speech of 30 July 1909 that Lloyd George began to change his tune, and to state privately that he might welcome the rejection of the Budget. 'I'm not sure we ought to pray for it to go through', he told the Mastermans at one of his breakfasts. 'I'm not sure we ought not to hope for its rejection. It would give us such a chance as we shall never have again'.

Whether or not the Lords rejected the 'People's Budget' when it first came up to them, the evidence is fairly conclusive that

Lloyd George wished land value taxation to become a permanent part of the British taxational system, and that he particularly wanted it for the purposes of reorganizing local finance. That land value taxation did not become a permanent part of British taxation as a consequence of his efforts was due, in the first instance, to his mismanagement of the Budget for 1914–15, and in the second instance to the political realignments brought about by the First World War.

Lloyd George, it is important to remember, had no training in matters of finance; he was what was known as a 'non-financial' Chancellor of the Exchequer. Indeed, when Asquith appointed Lloyd George to the Exchequer in April 1908, he did so with a good deal of reluctance and apprehension. His first inclination on succeeding Campbell-Bannerman as Liberal Prime Minister was to keep the Exchequer in his own hands or to give it to his Liberal Imperialist colleague, R. B. Haldane, but the political need to 'balance' his Cabinet and reassure the radicals of the party finally obliged him to award the Exchequer to Lloyd George.[2] So far from bringing with him to the Exchequer any fiscal expertise, Lloyd George impressed the Treasury officials as a virtual 'illiterate' in financial matters. According to the stories which emanated from Treasury sources in 1908, Lloyd George was 'absolutely without any arithmetical sense and found it quite impossible to understand the explanations of officials on financial matters'.[3] Arithmetic was never to prove Lloyd George's strong point, but the real trouble stemmed from his work methods, which jarred with the traditions of the Treasury. Treasury practice was to inform and enlighten ministers by written minutes, but Lloyd George simply refused to read anything properly, preferring as the radical journalist A. G. Gardiner wrote of him in 1908, to 'pick up a subject as he runs, through the living voice, never through books'. There was an essential lack of system in his approach. Lloyd George himself told George Riddell: 'I am like a hawk. I always swoop down on a thing. Sometimes I miss it, and then I have to go up and strike again'.

For all his lack of expertise and want of systematic approach to work, Lloyd George nevertheless proved enormously successful in providing for the national finances in accordance with Liberal free-trade principles. Confronted in his first year at the Exchequer with the unenviable task of having to meet an unprecedentedly large peace-time deficit of £16 million, he produced in response the 'People's Budget', which introduced the super tax and other direct

taxes aimed mainly at the rich. The new taxes were avowedly designed to expand with the expanding demands of the state; aided by
a revival in trade, that was precisely what most of them did, and it
did not again become necessary to introduce new taxation until
1914–15.

The only taxes introduced in the 'People's Budget' which did not
prove at all productive were the land value duties, notably a tax of
20% on the future 'unearned' increment in site values and a half-
penny tax in the pound on the site value of undeveloped land. Not
only were the yields of these duties small, but the considerable cost
of the land valuation they necessitated meant that they cost more
to raise than they provided in revenue. Lloyd George was warned
both by Sir George Murray, the Permanent Secretary of the Treasury,
and by his Cabinet critics that the land value duties would prove
impracticable and financially worthless, but was not deterred. For
him the land value duties were important not as a means of raising
revenue, but as a means around the veto of the Lords on the question
of land valuation. 'I knew the land taxes would not produce much',
he told Riddell in May 1912. 'I only put them in the Budget because
I could not get a valuation without them'.

When Lloyd George began the preparation of his Budget for
1909–10 it was perfectly clear that the Liberal Government could
not hope to carry their proposals for land valuation through the
Lords by normal procedures. In 1907 the Lords had rejected the
Government's Land Valuation (Scotland) Bill, and when it was
reintroduced in 1908 it was so badly mauled by the Lords that the
Government withdrew the measure. The only possible way of
'circumnavigating' the Lords was to provide for land valuation in a
Budget, in the anticipation that the Lords would hesitate to tamper
with a Finance Bill. In November 1908 a petition signed by 241
Liberal and Labour M.P.s was presented to Asquith by the Land
Values Group in Parliament urging that the next Budget incorporate
a national tax which would involve a national valuation, and it was
primarily as a means for securing valuation that Lloyd George
justified to the Cabinet his inclusion of land value duties in the
Budget for 1909–10. 'Enables us to legislate on one of the greatest
questions submitted to the country despite the House of Lords',
he jotted down in the outline notes of the case he put before the
Cabinet. 'This is really what makes our supporters so keenly desirous
for it'.[4]

Since the Liberal 'landslide' victory in the January 1906 general election, the Land Values Group in Parliament had constantly pressed the Government to legislate for land valuation and the separate rating of site values. The Group was an amalgam of land nationalizers, single taxers, and other less radical varieties of land taxers, bound together by their common need for land valuation, whether for the purpose of compulsory purchase or for that of land value taxation, and agreed on the necessity for introducing site value rating, although for different reasons. The Land Nationalisation Society, which claimed nearly 130 supporters in the House of Commons elected in 1906, was not really interested in site value rating for the purposes of relieving existing rates; its goal was to abolish private ownership in land and it wanted site value rating primarily to raise the funds for compulsory land purchase by local authorities. The goal of the single taxers, who owed their inspiration to the American, Henry George, was to shift the burden of all taxation, local and national, ultimately onto land values. Land values, they contended, represented a gift from the community to the landowners in that land values were the creation of society, and by taxing land values the community would merely be reclaiming for its own uses what it had created. A tax on land values was thus the fairest of all taxes – it deprived no individual of anything he had earned – and before resorting to other taxes, the community should exhaust the revenue-producing capacity of land values taxation. In part because of the importance they gave to freeing improvements from the burden of rates, and in part for tactical reasons, the single taxers had come, by the turn of the century, to make the introduction of site value rating the focus of their immediate campaign; by so doing they had struck up an alliance with the municipal groups intent on redistributing the burden of local taxation, and opening up a new source of revenue to local authorities by way of the separate rating of site values. In 1906 some 518 local authorities petitioned Campbell-Bannerman in favour of site value rating.

Rates in Great Britain were assessed on the annual present-use value of site and structures taken together, and in England and Wales they were the liability of occupiers rather than of both occupiers and owners, as was the case in Scotland. Rates, moreover, provided local authorities with their only source of local taxation, and with the rapid growth in local government expenditure in the late 19th and early 20th centuries, the pressure on rates was often enormous, particularly in the poorer districts. Relief to existing rates, and the equalization of the burden of local taxation, consequently stood at the core of the whole demand for the reform of local taxation and finance.

The simplest method of relieving rates, and of equalizing the burden of local taxation between rich and poor districts, was to increase Imperial subventions for the provision by local authorities of 'national' services, notably education and poor relief, and to revise the antiquated system by which these subventions were distributed. This, with variations, was the line of action recommended in the Final Report of the Royal Commission on Local Taxation in 1901. In the main, the commission saw only the difficulties in any radical overhaul of the system of local taxation, though in a Separate Report on Urban Rating and Site Values five of the commissioners recommended the introduction of a moderate rate on site values in urban areas to help meet local expenditure on urban improvements which increased the value of urban land. Such a rate, they contended, by enabling some of the burden of local taxation to be removed from improvements made on the site, would do 'something towards solving the difficult and urgent housing problem'.

It was precisely this latter point that was emphasized by the single taxers, and by land taxers generally. For them land values taxation was not simply, or even mainly, a fiscal expedient: it was a social reform. Indeed, it was a panacea. By placing a sufficiently high rate or tax on the capital value of all land, regardless of its present use or non-use, and by correspondingly de-rating buildings and other improvements, more land would be diverted onto the market, land prices would fall, building would boom, the housing shortage would be resolved, industry would be liberated and unemployment would recede. 'The chief object of the proposed taxation', C. P. Trevelyan explained to Campbell-Bannerman in a letter of October 1903, 'is to relieve buildings from their present enormous burden, whether they are used for industry or habitation. The help afforded would be not to one particular kind of manufacturers, but to all industries'.[5]

Although never a single taxer, Lloyd George, from the beginning of his political career, was a land taxer. Raised in what he later liked to describe as the 'blackest Tory parish' in Wales, he early acquired a prejudice against the Tory landlords of Wales, and in some of his first public speeches denounced the rating system as favouring the interests of landlords. Before becoming Chancellor of the Exchequer he had made land reform and taxation, the creation of a national system of education under popular control, and the curtailment of the drink traffic the focal points of his answer to the 'social question'.

In the autumn of 1908, when Lloyd George began the preparation of his first Budget, virtually his first decision was to include land value duties. Although his duties were radically revised in the Cabinet, and further diluted in the Commons, his main valuation proposals remained intact. As provided for by the Finance (1909–10) Act, 1910, the Commissioners of the Inland Revenue were to undertake a systematic valuation of all the land in the United Kingdom, showing the total value (including improvement) and the site value (minus improvements) on 30 April 1909 of every piece of land under separate occupation. In 1910 the Land Value Office of the Inland Revenue was set up, and Lloyd George announced that the process of valuation would be completed by 1915.

The Land Values Group, like Lloyd George, regarded the land value duties of the 'People's Budget' as useful primarily because of the national valuation they made possible; unlike Lloyd George, whose attention was taken up by the Lords issue and his scheme for national insurance, it was impatient for an immediate follow-up to the land value provisions of the Budget, and was appalled by the length of time allowed for carrying out the valuation. In May 1911 it presented Asquith and Lloyd George with a memorial, signed by 174 M.P.s, urging the speeding-up of the valuation and necessary legislation to empower local authorities to levy rates on the basis of the valuation, and in the next year it mounted a militant campaign for rating reform and full land values taxation. It feared that the Liberal Government would not resolve the rating issue before the next general election, due in 1915, and it suspected Lloyd George of dragging his feet on rating reform, despite his appointment in 1911 of a Departmental Committee on Local Taxation, under the chairmanship of Sir John Kempe. As A. C. Murray, the Liberal M.P. for Kincardineshire, saw the situation in July 1912, the land taxers were 'becoming more arrogant every day, one of them having the audacity to say that there was no place in the Liberal Party for anyone who did not accept their policy'. That policy, by 1912, called for both a uniform national tax levied on the new valuation, the proceeds of which were to be allocated to local authorities for the performance of 'national' services, and the imposition of a local rate on site values to finance mainly local services.

In June 1912 Lloyd George, with the next general election in view, returned to the land question, launching the Land Enquiry Committee to inquire into the land question in both its rural and urban aspects, and to formulate new policies in regard to land, housing and rating. The Committee's first thrust was an enquiry into the rural problem, and in October 1913 it published its rural report. At Bedford on 11 October Lloyd George formally opened his great land campaign.

The rural focus of Lloyd George's land campaign in 1913 outraged the land taxers, many of whom were now convinced that he was deliberately evading the issue of urban rating. 'His main appeal for *power*', Trevelyan wrote to Walter Runciman, the President of the Board of Agriculture, on the eve of the launching of the land campaign, 'must be to the towns . . . I can guarantee that the mass of land-taxers will swallow a good deal which they think heresy if rating of land values gets a real place. Otherwise I feel certain his campaign will go off in smoke'.[6] To Lloyd George he wrote on 2 November 1913: 'I want to urge you very strongly not to delay any longer declaring yourself in general terms at least in favour of land values as the proper basis of local rating. I don't think you can delay doing so without a good deal of misunderstanding arising. In a great many urban constituencies this is what they mean by land reform'.[7]

In fact, although Lloyd George was determined not to have his land campaign identified with the extremist notions of the single taxers, and although he sometimes spoke privately of his desire to 'twist the necks' of the single tax fanatics, he had no intention of evading the issue of land values taxation and rating reform. Throughout 1913 the Land Enquiry had been going 'very carefully' into the question of the rating and taxation of site values, and in September Lloyd George had raised the issue in the Cabinet. It was, as Riddell learned, with the 'great difference of opinion' in the Cabinet that his immediate difficulty lay. 'The knotty problem of rating', Runciman conceded in a letter to Lloyd George on 23 September, 'is likely to give us a lot of trouble'.

With a view to securing legislation in 1914, Lloyd George began in October 1913 to draw up alternative schemes for site value rating for the consideration of the Cabinet. These he put before the Cabinet in a memorandum on 13 December, and he also presented the case for a national tax on site values, the proceeds of which were to go to local authorities in relief of rates. 'During the last ten years, and especially as a result of the further knowledge gained from discussions upon the valuation under the Finance Act (1909–10), 1910', he asserted in his memorandum in support of site value rating in both rural and urban areas, 'the rating of site values is no longer regarded so much as a means of raising fresh revenue as a means whereby a stimulus can be given to the better use of land for productive purposes, whether such land be used for building or for agricultural purposes'. He sought to justify anew the national site tax, which the Cabinet had rejected in 1909, on the grounds that there was a general agreement that further grants must be made from the Exchequer in relief of rates, and that the only way to prevent owners of site values from gaining not only the general relief to rates common to all who shared in the payment of rates, but also from gaining an increase in their rent by the diminution of rates, was by a national tax on site values. Although the Cabinet showed itself no more willing than in 1909 to sanction a national site tax, Lloyd George was nevertheless able on 1 January 1914 to assure P. W. Raffan, the secretary of the Land Values Group, in an open letter that the Government definitely intended to use the valuation 'for the purpose of compelling the owners of sites which are not now bearing their share of local taxation, to contribute on the basis of the real value of their property'.

By late February 1914 Lloyd George and the Cabinet had reached some agreement on how to secure the differential rating of land and structures. At a meeting with Inland Revenue officials on 24 February Lloyd George explained the two main components to the proposed course of action. Firstly, a Rating Bill was to be prepared by Herbert Samuel, the new President of the Local Government Board, to provide among other things for the separate valuation of land and improvements for rating purposes. Secondly, additional grants-in-aid totalling £6 million, to be distributed so as to give the greatest proportion of relief to the most hard-pressed areas, would be made to local authorities in 1915–16 for education and other 'national' services, and the intention was that the resultant relief in rates should go towards improvements.[8]

To an extent that Lloyd George never fully appreciated, these proposals involved enormous procedural difficulties. To begin with, the far from complete valuation undertaken under the provisions of the

'People's Budget' would have to be adapted for rating purposes, and that in itself was an immense task. At a minimum the valuation would have to be brought up to date, and certain improvements included in the Budget's definition of site value would have to be excluded; beyond that there was the administratively and politically tricky question of reconciling a rating system based on annual present-use values and a valuation which established capital values. Further, as Edwin Montagu, the Financial Secretary to the Treasury, tried to impress on Lloyd George, there was the simple question of finding the parliamentary time to pass the complicated legislation the proposals necessitated. 'No one could have had the honour and pleasure of working with you without catching some of your indomitable optimism', he wrote to Lloyd George on 29 April, 'but I still feel that with the continually recurring excitements of Home Rule you will not get your Party to come to the House, and you will not get the House to sit late in the year in order to pass dull, technical Rating Reforms'.[9]

As in 1909, Lloyd George turned in 1914 to his Budget in order to negotiate some of the obstacles in his way; he intended that his Budget for 1914 should do for local taxation and finance what his 'People's Budget' had done for national taxation and finance, and that it should likewise serve as an effective counter to the political offensive of the Unionists. 'At Monday's dinner', he wrote to his brother on 11 March, 'I submitted to P.M. and the rest a great scheme of action centering around the Budget, for throwing out of gear the whole Tory line of battle. This view of it commended it to my colleagues who approve'. The Tory strategy, Lloyd George had told Percy Illingworth, the Liberal Chief Whip, soon after he had launched the land campaign, was 'to talk Ulster to the exclusion of land', and he had warned: 'If they succeed we are "beat" and beat by superior generalship'. The Budget would hopefully get some of the talk back to land at a juncture when Ulster and Home Rule were otherwise dominating political debate.

On 3 March the Kempe Committee had published its report on local taxation, recommending increased Exchequer grants-in-aid to local authorities. The majority group of seven recommended against, and the minority of six in favour of site value rating. Lloyd George ignored the findings of the majority on site value rating, and in his Budget preparation went beyond the Committee's recommendations and the proposals he had outlined in February for expanding and restructuring Exchequer grants to local authorities. The scheme he drew up provided for additional grants totalling £11 million in a full year, and for temporary grants of £2½ million in 1914–15 so as to bring the scheme within the compass of his current Budget. The operation of the whole scheme, including the distribution of the temporary grants, was made conditional on the passage of the Government's proposals for a national system of valuation for local taxation which would separate site and improvements for the purpose of favouring improvements in the relief to be afforded to rates and for the purposes of site value rating. As Lloyd George told the House of Commons, in what Churchill described as his 'slatternly and obscure' Budget speech of 4 May: 'We intend that the taxation of site values shall henceforth form an integral part of the system of local taxation'.

Lloyd George's taxation proposals in his Budget for 1914–15 were directed even more pointedly than his 1909 proposals at the people he liked to call 'the rich'; to finance his new grants, and the increased Naval vote, he resorted entirely to increases in income tax, super-tax and death duties. At first the Budget caused little stir. 'No one seems to care a rap for the rich', Churchill wrote to his wife on 4 May. On the next day he wrote: 'The Budget has been less ill received than I expected, but we have still to hear the squeals of the wealthy. The Tory party do not evidently relish fighting their battle'. In the event, the lead against the Budget was taken by the 'money-bags' in the Liberal Party; in June a Liberal 'cave' against the Budget was organized by Sir Richard Holt, a Liverpool shipowner, and Lloyd George, though 'disgusted with these rich men', became distinctly worried about the Budget's unpopularity in Liberal circles. He found, moreover, that he had badly underestimated the procedural difficulties his proposals involved; it became clear to him that there was no prospect whatsoever of securing the passage of a Rating Bill during the current session; the Inland Revenue advised that it would be impossible to distribute the temporary grants for 1914–15 on any basis other than existing rateable value, and in the Commons the Unionists planned to challenge the constitutionality of tacking what they alleged was a Local Government Bill onto a Finance Bill. On 22 June, at a midday meeting, the Cabinet decided to abandon the temporary grants, to deduct a penny from the proposed increase in the income tax, and to postpone the section of the Finance Bill dealing with permanent grants, and the Government's measures for valuation and rating reform, until later in the session. These changes were made, Asquith told the King, 'in view of the exigencies of time, and of the objections taken by influential supporters of the Government to the Chancellor of the Exchequer's proposals'. Later that afternoon, the Speaker of the Commons, in response to Unionist questions, gave his opinion that 'it would be desirable if possible to return to the older practice of confining the Finance Bill to the imposition of taxes and arrangements for dealing with the National Debt'. On the next day McKenna, the Home Secretary, told Riddell: 'The whole thing has been a shocking muddle'.

From that muddle the cause of site value rating never recovered. Because of the war the Government never proceeded with its plans for rating reform, and the land value duties of the 'People's Budget' were themselves to become victims of the war. The original valuation was indefinitely delayed, and the builders made a dead set against the land value duties which they claimed unfairly taxed their profits, destroyed confidence in land development, and were likely to retard reconstruction after the war. Part of the understanding between Lloyd George and the Unionists for the maintenance of his Coalition Government after the war was that the land value duties should be scrapped. In 1920 Lloyd George's Government duly repealed the land value duties, and the revenue collected was repaid to those who had contributed to it.

NOTES

1. See the diary of C. P. Ilbert, 29 March 1909, House of Commons Library MS 72; and Lloyd George to J. A. Spender, 16 July 1909, British Museum Add. MSS. 46388.
2. For the approach to Haldane, see Haldane to his mother, 17 March 1908, National Library of Scotland MSS. 5979.
3. Strachey to Rosebery, 23 July 1908, Strachey Papers S/12/7/12.
4. Lloyd George Papers C/26/1/2.
5. B.M. Add. MSS. 41231.
6. Trevelyan to Runciman, 18 September 1913, Runciman Papers.
7. Lloyd George Papers C/4/12/3.
8. Somerset House Library M3.3 and N22.1. The Inland Revenue records relating to Lloyd George's Budgets and still in the possession of Somerset House were made available to scholars for the first time in mid-1975.
9. Lloyd George Papers C/1/1/16.

LOCALITY AND METROPOLIS IN THE BRITISH EMPIRE:
A Note on some Connections Between the British North America Act (1887) and Gladstone's First Irish Home Rule Bill (1886)

Deryck Schreuder

> We admitted the reasonableness of that principle [of responsible government] and it is now coming home to us from across the seas.
>
> *Gladstone (8 April 1886), Irish home rule speech*

What can properly be called 'local' in the history of the British Empire? We might interpret 'locality' as the smallest constituent unit of the Empire; or we could cast it in terms of the environmental microcosm of a particular settlement community.[1] Alternatively we could, from the vantage-point of the metropolis, conceive of locality as nothing less than the regional polities of the Imperial periphery. Such localities evolved their own particular and peculiar history; but they were also shaped in their political and constitutional development by membership of an international Empire.[2]

Most obviously, there was then a fine network of constitutional connections between the colonial localities, in which forms of 'representative' and 'responsible' government evolved in patterns derivative of a common experience of association in the Empire. Professor Mansergh's massive study of *The Commonwealth Experience* (London, 1969) is rich in illuminating such constitutional cross-pollinations. Less directly, I would like to suggest there was also a flow of precedents from the regional localities themselves, educating the statesmen of the metropolis. The Liberal move to home rule for Ireland, to take one example – the 'governing passion' in English public life after 1886 – tapped this experience of Empire in a revealing fashion.

The connection is far from simple. It has to be stated firmly and immediately, that of course in the case of Irish home rule, Gladstone was propelled to his declaration by potent domestic and party-political factors, as well as by very specific Irish circumstances in the

1880s.[3] His politics were never those of the detached scholar, anyway, implementing abstract ideals.[4] Peel had taught him indelibly that 'the great art of government was to work by such instruments as the world supplies, controulling [sic] and overruling their humours'.[5] He had also learned in his Peelite years, as an early memorandum on colonies notes, that it 'is our true wisdom to see and know our circumstances, with their *potentialities* – these are the materials with which a man is to work'.[6] Most significantly, he ultimately saw his greatest political strength – as an autobiographical note of 1896 records – in being able to divine not merely the rightness of an issue, but also its 'ripeness'.[7]

Home rule for the Irish drew from a highly pragmatic short-term assessment of the issue, and also from a broad historical understanding of the Union, with all its 'potentialities'. It was here that the larger Gladstonian experience in dealing with nationality and local self-government – in the British Empire quite as much as in Europe – intruded upon his thinking, providing an intellectual framework of understanding for dealing with the deep political, cultural and social problems of Ireland. He offered this highly interesting 'catechism' to a correspondent who pondered on the rectitude of the policy of home rule for the Irish in the 1880s:

1. Study the abominable, the almost incredible history of the Union . . .
2. Soak and drench yourselves with the writings of Mr Burke on Ireland, especially on the Grattan Parliament (and) most of all his writings on the American War.
3. Look a little at the effects of Home Rule (a) in Europe (b) in the Colonies. (No man can refute my quotation from Duffy's article on Canada.)
4. Consider a little what is representation and what does it mean . . . [8]

Of this catalogue of 'influences', the Empire precedents would particularly appear to deserve scrutiny, for the colonial experience impinged on his Irish policy at no less than two important levels: the first was primarily moral and intellectual, one of perception and empathy; the other was essentially utilitarian and constitutional, relating to the mechanisms for devolving power from metropolis to 'locality'. Taken together, these influences would suggest that

Gladstone's 'Imperial education' was equal to, if not more important than, what J. L. Hammond termed his 'European sense' of nationality in the evolution of his home rule ideas.[9]

Well before the 1880s Gladstone had already come to a deep appreciation of the value of forms of local 'home rule' through responsible government in the colonies of settlement. His Peelite years had seen him move to an increasingly 'liberal' posture on colonial questions. By 1849, when he supported Molesworth and the radical colonial reformers' motion on 'better government in the colonies', and when he drafted a major (unpublished) manuscript on colonial policy, he had indeed constructed a subtle tripartite liberal theory on the metropolitan-colonial relationship.[10] The overall design was to move toward a 'liberal Empire' of settlement, worked out through the crucial issues of local 'self-government', colonial responsibility for local defence, and the development of local cultural institutions as the natural expression of the desires and values of the colonial society. It was a far from mechanistic view of colonial policy, carrying as it did the later hall-marks of Gladstonian liberalism. Under a broad devolutionist banner, that 'it is coming to be understood that affairs of the colonies are best transacted and provided for by the colonists themselves, as the affairs of England are best transacted by Englishmen', there lay the strongly moral supposition of educating colonists in their duties and responsibilities. For Gladstone's view of local government had strong Millite overtones of politics or government as education and edification. Indeed, he thought that local government 'lay at the root of all our national aptitudes, by teaching the art of government in various and limited, but effective forms, to those persons . . . who have an opening toward public life'.[11] Further, it established the basis of a moral polity, as 'the privileges of freedom and the burdens of freedom,' were inseparable – 'to bear the burden is as necessary as to enjoy the privilege'.[12] Lastly there was also the empirical factor that local self-government promoted fealty rather than rebellion in colonial hearts: 'We cannot stamp the image of England on the colonies like a coat of arms upon wax'. Only liberal devolution of power and responsibility would 'generate a sentiment of grateful attachment; then alone would 'they exult in the connection with England by ties implying no petty pride on one side, no subservience on the other, they will still look as like they can to the land where Churchyards contain the bones of their fathers'.[13]

The closer implications of Gladstone's views for British domestic problems of regionalism and local nationality in the Celtic regions have been little explored, although he himself indicated their importance in his first Irish home rule speech: 'The principle I am laying down, I am not laying down exceptionally for Ireland. It is the very principle upon which, within my recollection, we have not only altered, but revolutionised our method of governing the colonies'.[14] By this argument the development and challenge of local nationality in the Empire – whether it be in Ireland or in more distant settlement colonies – required more devolution, not less: 'England tried to pass good laws for the Colonies . . . but the Colonies said – 'We do not want good laws; we want our own'. We admitted the reasonableness of that principle, and it is now coming home to us from across the seas'. Where Ireland seethed with discontent in the 1880s, the settlement colonies – in Gladstone's perception, anyway – reflected a growing harmony in their relationship with the mother country. Canada, he argued, was a good example of how this had come about: 'liberal administration set free their trade . . . gave them popular and responsible government', and the result had been a formerly restless dominion now 'bound in affection to the Empire'. By a short leap of logic, these 'lessons' of Empire could apparently be safely brought back to the United Kingdom. When extensions in the powers of local government were being proposed for Ireland in 1882, Gladstone interestingly supported his Irish policy by Canadian precedent; he reminded a sceptical Queen Victoria that the 'self-government now practised in Canada, and generally viewed as safe, if not wholly unexceptional, was regarded in the first years of Mr Gladstone's Parliamentary life, as nothing less than fatal to the unity of the Empire'.[15] History had, in other words, taught the good sense of devolution.

But were such examples and precedents in fact directly applicable to the United Kingdom? Was Lord Granville not right in gently suggesting to his friend and premier in 1882 that Canadian examples were not, in truth, good supports for his argument? After all, Canada was 'nearly as independent as possible'.[16] To such interjections, Gladstone added that he was 'far from intending to imply that such Home Rule as prevails in Canada could safely or properly be extended to Ireland . . .'[17] What then did he mean to imply? The answer is complex but fascinating. He appears to have used the lessons of the Empire to establish the *principle* of the value of devolution, and also to direct attention to the *potentialities* of the situation; he drew from the history of responsible government, and his own role in it – particularly his old concern for a separation of powers – to connect colonial 'home rule' to Irish devolution; and last of all, he extracted from the practical evolution of government in the colonies, especially Canada, useful working draft blue-prints which could be used in one way or another, when it came to devising home rule legislation within the United Kingdom.

There are several ways in which this can be shown, but two would appear to be most useful here. The form of home rule which Gladstone wished to implement for Ireland was much inspired by his concern for local autonomy through a jurisdictional division of powers, in the settlement Empire. It was as a colonial reformer that he had first pressed for such a separation of Imperial and colonial powers in the advances towards responsible government – 'I admit this cannot perfectly be effected by catalogue . . . [but] why not admit what can be done . . . by enumerating, then taking a general power for subjects of Imperial concern, solemnly adjudged by a high judicial authority like the Judicial Committee of the Privy Council'[19] – and who now, in 1886, advocated Irish home rule on the basis of an 'Irish Chamber for Irish affairs', 'equitable division of Imperial charges by fixed proportions', and 'suspension of Imperial authority for all civil purposes whatever'.[20] It was the old ally of Molesworth, the active debater over Australian and New Zealand Government Bills and Canadian tariffs, and the author of the Pretoria and London Conventions with the recalcitrant Boers of the African highveld – which granted the 'Transvaal State' internal self-government under the British flag and a general 'suzerainty' – who indeed wished to retain the Imperial veto over reserved subjects in the actual first home rule bill.[21] 'What I say on Ireland is simply an adaptation of what I have already often said', as Gladstone was at pains to explain to Lord Hartington in 1885, 'namely, that Ireland may have all that is compatible with the unity of the Empire'.[22] In short, home rule 'at home' was to be more limited than in the Imperial-colonial relationships, but it was to draw from the same principle. Thus, far from trying to obliterate all Anglo-Irish ties inherent in the Union, he merely wished, in his own words, to 'establish by statute a legislative body to sit in Dublin, and to deal with Irish as distinguished from Imperial affairs; in such a manner as would be just to each of the three kingdoms . . . and calculated to support and consolidate the unity of the empire on the continued basis of Imperial authority and mutual attachment'.[23]

The first home rule bill expressed these limited devolutionist intentions; and the general election of 1886 gave tangible sign, Gladstone believed, that this could form the basis of a new Anglo-Irish relationship, on a revised and special pattern – albeit adapted to suit the United Kingdom – derivative of the historical experience of the liberal Empire overseas. 'What does Ireland say?' he wrote in an open letter to Sydney Buxton, on 29 June 1886 (and subsequently published in the *Standard* a few days later), 'By mouth, 85 out of 101 of her popular representatives she declares herself content with this [Imperial] supremacy. She leaves you what is good in the Union, and she asks to be rid of what is bad. She asks you to do for her what you did with such advantage for Frenchmen in Canada, Dutchmen at the Cape, for the children of convicts in Tasmania – to give her management, not of English, or of Scotch, or of Imperial, but that of Irish affairs'.[24]

The Gladstone Papers in the British Museum also tell us much of how Gladstone actually prepared to draft the first Irish home rule bill.[25] If there was little in a direct constitutional sense to be taken from the workings of the actual metropolitan-colonial connection, in which the 'Dominions' were all to independent, there was still much useful material in the constitutions of these settlement societies. The Papers show that Gladstone was in possession of extensive memoranda on the colonies, drawn up by Robert Meade at the colonial office, including a 'secret' minute on responsible government in Victoria, South Australia, Tasmania, the Cape, New South Wales, New Zealand, Canada and Natal, with special emphasis given to defining the powers of the executive. Gladstone was also supplied with printed notes on the various classes of overseas legislatures: those with elected or nominated upper houses, and those with single houses. Given that he was particularly interested in regional autonomy in the larger dominions, this also naturally led him to consider, in detail, the British North America Act of 1867.

Gladstone's degree of interest in the B.N.A. Act is excellently revealed in the close working, marginalia, and amendments, to which he subjected his copy of the document.[26] He appears to have studied the B.N.A. Act line by line, as he worked out in his own mind how he would draft devolutionist legislation for Ireland. In one place, 'Section III' of the Act, which was concerned with the Executive Powers, 'Canada' is merely struck out and 'Ireland' inserted. Thus the reworked section came to look like this, with the deleted words in brackets, and the addition in italics:

9. The Executive Government and Authority of and over (Canada) *Ireland* is hereby declared to continue and be vested in the Queen.
10. The Provisions of this Act referring to the Governor-General extend and apply to the (Governor General) *Viceroy* for the time being . . .
    There shall be a council to aid and advise Government of (Canada) *Ireland* to be styled the Queen's Privy Council . . .

Gladstone's general working of this copy of the B.N.A. Act suggests that what attracted him to the document was not so much Imperial-colonial relations, but dominion-provincial relationships *in* Canada itself. Here, clearly, Canadian federalism was full of useful con-stitutional precedents, with its stress on the supremacy of the Domin-ion powers over the Provinces, and its careful division of powers between 'metropolis' and 'locality' in the confederation.[27] It would appear that, in this context, Gladstone was particularly drawn to Clause 91 of the B.N.A. Act – the powers of the Dominion parlia-ment, with its general statement of the supremacy of the Senate and House of Commons of Canada, together with its designated list of 'all matters coming within the Classes of Subjects herein after enumerated' (the 28 such reserved subjects). A 'secret' memorandum of 20 March 1886, on the planned Irish government bill has, fasci-natingly, written alongside the proposed executive powers, margi-nalia to the effect: 'Extent of legislative power, from "The British North America Act, 1867, section 91 . . ." '; and on the extent of executive power, 'See Canada (B.N. America) Act, sec. 9'. The second draft of the working basis of the bill, of 31 March 1886, also has this confirming note on the matter of legislative powers: 'The words preceding are *mutatis mutandis* from "the British North America Act, 1867", Section 91'.[28] Given the drift of his constitu-tional concerns, Gladstone must surely also have considered with close interest Clause 92 – the Executive Powers of the Provincial Legislatures' (15 defined 'Classes', plus 'Generally all Matters of a merely local or private Nature in the Province') – as well as Clauses 93 to 101, which set out the questions of 'Education', 'Uniformity of Laws', 'Agriculture and Immigration' and the 'Judicature' in a federalist polity. Clearly what he found attractive in the B.N.A. Act was what moved him away from the American constitution (which he also had to hand): Gladstone wished to establish the supremacy of the Imperial parliament, with a firm division of powers devolved upon the local authorities.[29]

If Canada and the British North American experience had initially helped to educate the young Peelite Gladstone in the constitutional advance of liberty by responsible local government, and the consequent adjustments of metropolis and colony in the era of Durham, Peel and Russell, so too the making of its 'home grown' federalist constitution had later come to the metropolitan centre to provide a useful working basis in devising new devolutionist legislation. The making of a 'liberal Empire', of responsible self-government, had *not* determined the coming or timing of Irish home rule.[30] For that we must look to domestic political issues, Irish history and the evolving Gladstonian appreciation of nationality as vested in tenant-right in Ireland.[31] But the history of decentralization and devolution in the metropolitan-colonial relationships had played an important role in helping Gladstone on towards home rule for the Irish; both by principle and precept Empire devolution was active in the liberal domestication of colonial home rule. Moreover, having made a commitment to constitutional readjustment in recognition of Irish 'nationality' – beyond mere amplification of the powers of existent local government structures in Ireland, as Chamberlain desired – then Gladstone found additional uses for the constitutions of the 'responsibly governing' colonial localities, especially the federalist foundations of the B.N.A. Act.[32]

If Imperial precedent and historical analogy had proved to be a valuable factor in enlarging Gladstone's understanding of Irish policy, it could also of course be argued that, in certain senses, it also concurrently limited his perception of Irish nationalism. Put very shortly, one result of his reading of the lessons of responsible government overseas, notably as it had evolved in Canada, was a faith that local nationality and 'colonial nationalism' were compatible with the Imperial connection; and that the only substantive issue at stake was how to devise a separation of powers which would both meet demands for local autonomy and recognize the interests of the Empire. With Mill, he accepted the notion of a 'second identity' for citizens of the Empire: Quebecers, Boers and Irishmen could both be true to their cultural roots *and* also enjoy the advantages of membership of an international association of states under the British flag. Separatist nationalism, the spirit of Sinn Fein and Afrikaner republicanism, were not received with any warmth by Gladstone, despite his avowed liberationist tendencies. Further, by perceiving federalist solutions to United Kingdom problems through the particular lens of the Canadian experience, he tended to see home rule in terms of devolution from the centre, rather than the creation of plural polity, with equal status for each of the member communities. As Parnell was to find in 1886, the Liberal leader felt quite able to devise home rule legislation without close consultation with the leader of the Irish home rule party.

Lord Salisbury once remarked on the possibility that it was Irish home rule which had awoken the slumbering giant of Imperial sentiment among the British people. This note suggests that his aphorism might just as well be stood on its head. It was, arguably, the colonial Empire itself, and the historical precedents which it offered in constitutional matters, which first began the Gladstonian education toward home rule in its many manifestations. As we discover the diversity of the Empire, through discrete national and local studies, we should be careful not to neglect the themes common to its extraordinary history. This would seem particularly true with respect to responsible government and devolution of power, in which there were many lessons to be learnt by the metropolis from the politics of the localities. Perhaps the child was, after all, father to the man.

NOTES

1. See for example, R. E. Frykenburg, *Guntur District, 1788-1848, a history of local influence and central authority in South India* (Oxford, 1965); and Sir Keith Hancock, *Discovering Monaro: a study of man's impact on the environment* (Cambridge, 1972).
2. See for example, W. A. Maxwell, 'The Cape of Good Hope', in *The Encyclopedaedia Britannica* (1963; rev. ed., 1971), vol. iv, pp. 816-25; and T. R. H. Davenport, 'The Consolidation of a New Society – the Cape Colony' in *The Oxford History of South Africa* (edited by Monica Wilson and Leonard Thompson, Oxford, 1969). vol. 1 pp. 272-333.
3. A. B. Cooke and John Vincent, *The Governing Passion: Cabinet Government and Party Politics in Britain, 1885-8* (Harvester Press, 1974), esp. pp. 51-66, and D. A. Hamer, *Liberal Politics in the Age of Gladstone and Roseberry. A Study in Policy and Leadership* (Oxford, 1972).

4. H. C. G. Matthew, 'Introduction', to *The Gladstone Diaries* (Oxford, 1974), vol. iii, pp. xli-xlii; and D. A. Hamer, 'Understanding Mr Gladstone', *The New Zealand Journal of History*, vol. 6, no. 2, Oct. 1972, pp. 115–128.

5. Gladstone Memorandum, 26 April 1844 (Gladstone Papers, British Museum, 44777 ff. 172–5) printed in J. Brooke and M. Sorensen (eds.), *The Prime Ministers Papers: W. E. Gladstone, Autobiographical Memoranda, 1832–45* (London, 1972), ii, p. 164.

6. Gladstone Memorandum, 9 June 1840 (44819 ff. 49–51) quoted *ibid.*, 121.

7. R. T. Shannon, *The Crisis of Imperialism* (London, 1974), pp. 71–2.

8. 44548 f. 106 (Gladstone to R. H. Hutton).

9. On Gladstone's 'European sense' see J. L. Hammond, *Gladstone and the Irish Nation* (London, 1938), chap. V; on the colonial dimension of home rule ideas, P. Knaplund, *Gladstone and Britain's Imperial Policy* (London, 1927; reprinted 1966), pp. 38–94.

10. W. E. Gladstone, unpublished MS., 'Memorandum on Colonies' (c. 1848–9), 44738 ff. 234–63.

11. Gladstone to Granville, 5 Oct. 1885 in Agatha Ramm (ed.), *The Political Correspondence of Mr Gladstone with Lord Granville 1876–86* (OUP 1962) vol. ii, p. 403.

12. Select Committee on Colonial Military Expediture ('Mills Committee') *Parliamentary Papers, 1861*, XIII, no. 423; question 3781.

13. 'Memorandum on colonies', *op. cit.*, f. 249.

14. The home rule speech is in *Hansard* (3) cciv, debate of 8 April 1886; cols. 1081–5 are especially pertinent to our theme here.

15. Gladstone to Queen Victoria 13 Feb. 1882, G. E. Buckle (ed.), *Letters of Queen Victoria* (London, 1926), 2nd Ser., iii, pp. 260–2.

16. Granville to Gladstone, 13 Feb. 1882, Ramm, *Gladstone-Granville correspondence*, i, 341.

17. Gladstone to Queen, *op. cit.*

18. Gladstone Memorandum 12 Dec. 1854 on 'reserved powers' in responsible government, 44744 f. 131. *Hansard* (3) CV, 959–60, for Gladstone support of Molesworth and statement on jurisdictional division of powers.

19. 44585 f. 81 (Cabinet Memorandum).

20. Gladstone to Herbert Gladstone, 14 Nov. 1885. Quoted Hammond, *Gladstone and the Irish Nation*, p. 448.

21. For example see Gladstone to Lord Lyttleton, 2 May 1846, 44528 f 41; also 44744 ff. 125–33, 44585 f. 81, and 44738 ff. 87–109, for detailed notes on Australian bill. Knapland, *Gladstone's Imperial Policy*, pp. 103–21 gives a succinct account. See also *Hansard* (3), clxxxvi col. 756; Gladstone to Queen Victoria, 28 Oct. 1892, *Letters of Queen Victoria* (3) ii, 172–3; and D M Schreuder, *Gladstone and Kruger: Liberal Government and Colonial 'Home Rule' 1880–85* (London, 1969).

22 Gladstone to Hartington 11 Sept. 1885. Quoted Hammond, *Gladstone and the Irish Nation*, p. 406.

23. Gladstone Cabinet Memorandum, Jan. 1886, in Morley, *Gladstone*, iii, p. 292. Also, Gladstone to Bright, 14 May 1886, 44548 f. 88.

24. Gladstone to Sydney Buxton, 29 June 1886, 44548 f. 106.

25. See volumes 44632 and 44633 (British Museum).

26. The B.N.A. Act is also summarized on 10 Downing Street note paper ff. 107–111) in another hand.
27. See R. M. Dawson, *The Government of Canada* (Toronto, 1956), pp. 33–5 and 608–13.
28. 44632, ff. 189–94.
29. He also possessed notes on prerogatives of the crown, drawn from Elackstone (*Ibid.*, ff. 137–8) and on prerogatives of the crown in colonial bills (ff. 138–9).
30. The actual final drafts of the Irish home rule bill are in 44633 ff. 4–31.
31. See E. D. Steele, *Irish Land and British Politics: Tenant-right and Nationality 1865–70* (Cambridge, 1974), esp. pp. 104–9, on the influence of Indian land legislation as discussed in the writings of George Campbell.
32. Gladstone to R. H. Hutton, 44548 f. 106, and Gladstone to Chamberlain, 5 May 1885, 44548 f. 12.

WEST INDIAN ANGLICAN COMMUNITIES
Seen Through the Eyes of
two Victorian Ladies

June Williams

Bundles of crossed letters in sloping feminine handwriting among the Rawle papers in Rhodes House Library, Oxford, bring to life the daily round of two Anglican communities in the West Indies in the second half of the 19th century.[1] The papers (MSS W. Ind. s. 41) are centred on the activities of the Reverend Richard Rawle, Principal of Codrington College, Barbados (1846–63) and Bishop of Trinidad (1872–88). With few exceptions the collection does not stem directly from Rawle himself, but dates from his marriage in January 1851 to Susan Ann Blagg of Cheadle, his old parish in Staffordshire, and, during the years in Barbados, consists mainly of her letters to her aunt, Miss Harriet Blagg. Between 1855 and 1864 these are supplemented by letters from Mrs M. C. Layton, widow of a West Indian vicar and headmistress of the girls' school on the Codrington Estates, who seems to have adopted Miss Blagg as her 'aunt' after accompanying the Rawles on a visit to England.

Codrington College was founded in 1710 by Christopher Codrington for 'the study and practice [of] Physic and Chirurgery as well as Divinity' under the auspices of the Society for the Propagation of the Christian Religion in Foreign Parts. Financial vicissitudes, hurricane disasters, and a basic shortage of raw material in the shape of suitably educated local scholars had from time to time led to deviations from the Founder's original purpose of training medical missionaries. The school for boys which had of necessity developed as a subsidiary part of the establishment had, since the end of the 18th century, become a substitute for the theological college it had been created to feed: promising scholars were sent to England at the Foundation's expense for further training, not necessarily for holy orders. In 1829 the Bishop of Barbados had joined with the Society in reconstituting the Foundation in accordance with the Founder's design; but Rawle's arrival in 1847 coincided with a movement among the island's upper classes to revert to the pre-1829 situation. By 1851 Rawle had not only defeated this attempt to undermine the

theological nature of the establishment, but was planning to increase
student accommodation and to train missionaries for West Africa,
in addition to improving the day schools for the children of workers
on the Codrington Estates.

Both Mrs Rawle and Mrs Layton were involved not only in teaching in the girls' school, but also in the church, Sunday school and
choral work centred on the College and the Society's chapel. Their
letters give in minute detail a picture of their everyday domestic
lives and routine duties against a background of tiredness and ill-
health, accentuated, in the Principal's case especially, by systematic
overwork in a trying climate. Partly because of a chronic shortage
of satisfactory helpers, and partly for the sake of economy (a pressing
need at this time of general depression in the West Indies and of
financial difficulties for the Society and the Codrington Fund)
Rawle was, in addition to his duties as Principal of the College and
Lecturer in Divinity, acting as the Chaplain to the College and Estates,
lecturing in mathematics, and assisting with the teaching in the
Society's boys' school throughout much of this period. He also re-
organized the boys' school at the College, and advised on the reorganization and staffing of schools in Bridgetown. To this load he
subsequently added the training of pupil-teachers and of missionaries.
Ill-health forced him to abandon his intention of leading the mission
to West Africa himself, but its progress is a recurrent theme in the
letters of this period: it is clear that Rawle was deeply involved in
the preliminary planning, the training and selection of personnel,
producing vernacular texts for the mission's use and in organizing
the fund-raising activities that made it possible. Fund-raising, not
only for the mission, was an ever-present problem. Characteristically, throughout his term of office Rawle was planning and personally supervising extensions and improvements to the College, Chapel
and school buildings. As the letters show, these activities were financ-
ed to some extent by local support, substantially by the Rawles themselves, and also by friends and relations in England.

Following Rawle's resignation for health reasons in 1863 there is
a gap in the collection coinciding with a nine-year period spent in
England, first in convalescence, then as Vicar of Tamworth. The
sequence of letters is resumed three years after his consecration as
Bishop of Trinidad in 1872. With the exception of two letters to Aunt
Harriet (who died in 1881) they are exclusively from Mrs Rawle to
her sister-in-law Fanny (Mrs Charles John Blagg, also of Cheadle).

There is no reference to Mrs Layton, who in January 1864 had been planning to follow the Rawles to England.

Against a background of domestic gossip about family and friends in England and about Trinidad personalities, a picture emerges of the tasks confronting Rawle in a new diocese carved out after the disestablishment of the Anglican Church in the West Indies and insufficiently provided for. For reasons of economy as well as personal preference Rawle abjured episcopal state, lived in the rectory attached to the parish church of Holy Trinity, Port-of-Spain, and combined the duties of parish priest and hospital chaplain with his diocesan work. In a climate infinitely more trying than that of Barbados, and without the opportunity of annual leave, the Bishop, his curates and the rest of the island's clergy were continually hampered in their duties by the effects of endemic fever aggravated by overwork due to a shortage of suitable incumbents. There were also grave disciplinary problems, some of which Rawle was able to solve by persuading the Church Council to re-frame the canons in 1883. Despite these difficulties he embarked with characteristic vigour on a programme of mission work among the Indian and Chinese communities, and of church and school building, ranging from the transformation of Holy Trinity into the Cathedral to the literal propping-up of St. Augustine's, a country church subsiding on its foundations of pitch. He was constantly on tour (not scorning donkey-back when necessary), supervising and consecrating these works, standing in for absent clergy, and carrying out confirmations. Both he and Mrs Rawle saw the religious education of the island's youth as a major challenge. Mrs Rawle's duties – her Saturday classes for girls, her working parties, her parish tasks linked with the cycle of church festivals, her work for religious and charitable organizations – were supplemented by the constant obligation to provide hospitality to clerical and lay visitors. 'Our beds are kept well-aired', she commented drily in 1882. Sometimes their occupants had fever or were otherwise afflicted: 'the spare bedroom has been a hospital on many occasions'. Even such social distractions as are mentioned – amateur readings, performances of *Patience* and *Elijah* – were seen mainly in terms of raising money for church work; and time was found to support (with some reservations) the temperance movement and to start a parish magazine. Although her concern for her ageing husband's health dominates the letters of this period, her own health was suffering too: she died of heart failure while on leave in England in 1883. Her husband, unable to carry on without her support, resigned from the Bishopric in the same year and went back to Barbados as Honorary Principal to Codrington, where he died in May 1889.

The letters are valuable source material for historians interested in local and social history. The minutiae of daily life, the atmosphere and tone of the two communities, are revealed through the eyes of two feminine observers very different in type but wholly characteristic of their period. Often it is not so much what is recorded as the attitude of the writer that is revealing: the limitations of outlook are as illuminating as the content. But even if the letters are of limited value for reflecting life in Barbados and Trinidad generally, there is, to counter-balance this, the unusual advantage that, for the Codrington period, two observers are simultaneously recording their impressions of that community through very different eyes. The letters sent off by the regular 'packet' to Miss Blagg, The Terrace, Cheadle, very often shared the same envelope, but the two writers, though superficially sharing the same culture, were not of the same background or temperament.

For Mrs Rawle, daughter of one of Rawle's most active parishioners in Cheadle, life as the helpmeet of the Principal of Codrington, subsequently the Bishop of Trinidad, seems to have been the natural extension of her family's involvement in parish activities. The setting, admittedly, was a little different – she occasionally complains of the shortage of 'suitable greens' for Christmas and Easter decorations; thinks wistfully of the English spring, so much more seasonable a background to Easter than Trinidad's unnatural brightness; and comments from Port-of-Spain in 1881:

> The Public here keep Xtmas [sic] in the most senseless fashion; they let off crackers and rockets and other fireworks . . . in the streets and make all manner of noises the whole night . . . but there is no carol singing, or anything of that kind.

But, although she wrote of her first Christmas at Codrington 'Nothing can be more un-Christmaslike than this day has seemed to me', she continued significantly 'except in Chapel when one might shut one's eyes and hear the words of the service so often listened to before and fancy oneself in the old corner in Cheadle Church'. Church and parish activities were at once a means of adjusting to her new environment and a link with home. Her letters frequently refer to parish activities and personalities at Cheadle and clearly she conducted parish affairs at Codrington exactly as she would have done at home – but there were difficulties peculiar to the colonial environment: the children at the Monday evening singing, for example, found it difficult to master chants, but eventually made some progress with 'Jerusalem' and 'Dundee', and the singing in chapel was, by 1859, 'at any rate congregational and hearty'. According to Mrs Layton, always a more sweeping critic, the congregation tended to overdo the finery, local masons were 'not quite up to Church building in a proper style', and communicants approached the Lord's Table too lightly; while Rawle's theological students and confirmation candidates seem often to have been unsatisfactory. But, despite these snags, the parish routine at Codrington and later at Port-of-Spain might have been that of any English parish, with working parties for ladies, morning classes for working girls and afternoon classes for upper-class children, Christmas trees and dinners for the poor, the Sisters' Association and the Daily Meals Society – though the Young Women's Help Society was one charity Mrs Rawle found local sentiment in Port-of-Spain unwilling to accept. Above all there was the everlasting business of raising money for school, mission and parish through church sales, magic lantern shows, readings, tableaux, and, more daringly, oratorios and amateur productions of Gilbert and Sullivan. Money-raising was a strong link with the home parish; family and friends contributed not only in money but in kind. 'I am glad Alice is getting on well with the missionary basket' wrote Mrs Rawle from Trinidad, evoking, in one sentence, the whole atmosphere of Victorian good works which she was engaged in transplanting to a Caribbean setting.

Moments of private relaxation, too, were very much what they would have been at home:

> I am not long got up from the harmonium, for I generally play to 'the old man' a little while he rests on the sofa after dinner, and among other things have been playing 'Sound the loud timbrels' which always reminds me of Aunt Kate.

The 'calico balls' and other diversions that blossomed when the fleet was in at Port-of-Spain were too dashing for the Rawles. 'We don't enter into it . . . There has been a great deal of gaiety lately, but Lent will put a stop to it' she concludes triumphantly, though an occasional note of wistfulness is also to be detected. Normally forced to content herself with amateur productions, she had her more

exciting moments. 'We are actually going to an entertainment
tonight, the Bishop too! . . . A recital of Musical and Intellectual
Treats'. And in 1886 she confessed to going to two 'rather superior'
productions by a professional touring company. But tolerance stop-
ped short at the more indigenous entertainments:

> This is the Carnaval [*sic*] time, most disagreeable! nothing but
> stupid idiotic noises in the streets . . . they don't do any harm,
> except that everybody is idle . . . [and] . . . making fools of
> themselves.

Like so many Englishwomen abroad, Mrs Rawle made few concessions to her environment, looking at it very much through English
eyes. It is significant that in one of her rare descriptive passages
praising local scenery the adjective she chooses is 'park-like'. She
was not wholly able to ignore climatic differences, admitting that
'one feels the want of bracing', which is hardly surprising, since she
continued to wear flannel, attributing her immunity from chills to
this habit. Determined to keep up other British habits conducive to
health, she reported proudly that people said of her 'Ah she must be
mad, she takes such walks': but by 1859 she confessed 'One can
only walk comfortably in the evening . . . tho' I always go out every
day, which is not the rule in the West Indies'; and she later compro-
mised and took to riding. She does seem to have recognized that
some adjustment to the new environment was necessary. Describing
a new bride, she says somewhat scornfully 'I don't know how she
will get on here, she made a great piece of work at the sight of an
ant one day'. She herself was nothing if not strong-minded, and a
woman of resource, as we learn from Mrs Layton, for 'finding a large
crab in the diningroom, which ran into the harmonium towards her,
she began to play, thinking it would come out'. When warning her
aunt to expect certain short-comings should she visit them at Codrington, she added '. . . there is nothing in the world, unless people
are determined to be discontented, to prevent anyone from being
very comfortable here'. Throughout her stay in the West Indies she
kept up this strong-minded attitude. Later on, in Trinidad, she did
confess that she would have preferred the Bishop to be at home
during the hurricane of 1878, and complained on rare occasions of
mosquitoes and dust, but she qualified this by reporting, after the
rains, 'The climate here is delicious now'.

Mrs Layton was a very different sort of person. Though professing admiration for Mrs Rawle's stoical behaviour, she was herself much more volatile, and had, in Mrs Rawle's words, 'not much control over her feelings . . . I can always be calm and cool myself so that I cannot quite sympathise'. It is tempting to attribute this difference in character to the differing origins of the two ladies. Although Mrs Layton had relatives in England most of her family appear to have lived in Barbados and other West Indian islands, and the visit she paid to England with the Rawles appears to have been her first. She had clearly received a good education on English lines, and had presumably experienced the life of an Anglican vicar's wife (though little of what she refers to as 'my painful history' is known to us). She constantly emphasizes her social and cultural links with Britain: she reads *The Daisy Chain*, *Jane Eyre*, Dickens and Trollope in monthly parts; urges Miss Blagg to send her pressed violets and primroses to remind her of the English spring; and reports visits by Barbadian friends and connections to Malvern to take the waters and to London for the Exhibition. Speaking of the Mutiny, she says

> What a miserable war this has been – and I am afraid we deserve it all . . . I say *we*, for you know we Barbadians, always being famed for our loyalty, consider ourselves as English as you are.

But however English Mrs Layton may have felt herself to be, being in fact of Barbadian origin she was naturally able to identify with the island in a way that Mrs Rawle was not. In consequence, a rather more vivid picture both of Codrington and, to some extent, of Barbados emerges from her letters. She is much more involved with her environment; rejoices in the sugar harvest and its pleasures; takes an almost child-like delight in sending her English friends calabashes and other West Indian curiosities, together with assorted specimens of local flora (an interest shared to some extent by Mrs Rawle, who found that local shrubs and lilies survived the attention of 'fowls and Parasole ants' better than English mint); describes in detail her everyday life and doings, her pupils, and her difficulties with them; and reports on local events and entertainments, weddings and christenings in particular, for which she enjoys dressing up, though this does not prevent her from criticizing 'the lower order of whites' for taking the same pleasure – 'How sad it is to see the love of dress so common in the female mind'. She speaks with relish of gaieties following the arrival of the 49th Regiment, and of marriages between its officers and West Indians – 'a nice chance for our young ladies' – and does not altogether succeed in concealing behind the veneer of Victorian English moralizing, which she sometimes carries to excess, a quality of worldliness which makes her a useful reporter of the local scene, though her use is limited by the circumstances of her life at Codrington, by her outlook and by the effect she is aiming to create in her letters to Miss Blagg, which inevitably inhibit their spontaneity.

The letters reflect the racial and social pattern of life in the British West Indies with perhaps the difference that at Codrington the races are rather more closely associated than is normal. There are what Mrs Layton describes as 'the lower orders', servants and plantation workers, mainly black with a coloured admixture, whose children she teaches; the pupils, drawn from all races, of the Lodge School and the College; the teaching staff, recruited mainly from England; and, in the wider community surrounding Codrington, there are contacts (rather few) with Government House and the official establishment; with plantation owners and managers, merchants and others living in Bridgetown, some of them Mrs Layton's relatives; and, naturally with other Anglican clergy (though Mr. Rawle's relations with the Bishop of Barbados, exacerbated by the appointment of the Bishop's son as College Tutor, are reminiscent of those between Archdeacon Grantly and Bishop Proudie). The society revealed is stratified economically, racially and socially, and the stratification is accepted without question, terms like 'the lower orders' being used quite unselfconsciously to describe the economically less fortunate (usually black, sometimes coloured, occasionally white). Mrs Rawle's use of terms like these is always more charitable, less pejorative; her social assumptions are perhaps less overt than Mrs Layton's. 'I wish you could see me escorting 20 girls as black as ink', the latter writes, emphasizing her racial status in a way which makes one wonder whether she was a Creole, though her motive may simply have been to underline her identity with the culture represented by Miss Blagg in contrast to that represented by her pupils – a motive familiar enough in those of colonial origin drawn culturally to the colonial power. She makes many explicit references to race and colour – 'the black children are so afflicted with stubbornness' – 'the black mind will not study'. It is the coloured children whom she makes monitors, though she has problems with them too, and she dismisses an unsatisfactory student as 'No use to us. He was coloured'. Yet she is capable, also, of describing another student as 'a gentleman of colour', and of turning right round and admitting

> With all our boasting, poor Barbados is very far behind in
> educational matters. The blacks under Mr Rawle's care are
> *very* superior to the whites in the island.

It is, however, important not to infer too much from these letters
scribbled hurriedly to catch the outgoing packet, with their contra-
dictions and swings of mood natural in someone of Mrs Layton's
temperament. It is scarcely surprising that, coping almost single-
handed with a crowded school, she sometimes felt despondent and
wrote critically about her pupils, and it is only natural that, being
a Victorian, it did not occur to her politely to evade the question of
colour.

Coming from outside the island, Mrs Rawle could take a more
unbiased view. 'The Rawles tell me' wrote Mrs Layton 'that the
English people of the lower class, are far more troublesome than
our folk'. Mrs Rawle's attitude to her servants and dependants
seems to have been sympathetic; after an absence in England she
speaks of 'our poor people' welcoming them with gifts on their
return. Occasionally there is a touch of condescension that grates on
the modern ear:

> I dont think . . . that you will despise our little blackies when
> you see our 300 infants all in their gallery, nice, intelligent little
> faces some of them have & are most lovable little things and I
> can assure . . . anyone that desires to disparage the negroes that
> many of our school-children would put to shame the children in
> English schools,

though some, she confesses, are 'at first sight somewhat repugnant
to a European'. She was, like Mrs Layton, alive to the sufferings of
the labouring classes, especially during the depression, and to their
treatment by the plantation managers, but records the dilemma into
which her sympathies lead her:

> . . . the people are so lazy they will make every excuse for not
> working, while the manager cannot get things done on the estate
> for want of labour, yet the people do often . . . really want at the
> time they come to beg, yet if one gives to all, the whole popula-
> tion of the estate would be upon us, & yet it seems hard to turn
> them away.

'The people' is a characteristic euphemism; overt references to
colour are comparatively rare in Mrs Rawle, though she does comment with unusual sharpness on one or two mixed marriages, and
criticizes a missionary's bride for dressing unsuitably 'just like the
coloured young when raised a little'. On the whole, however, her
attitude does credit to the wife of a Christian minister: 'a glorious
day for the poor negroes' she exclaims 'when the first *black* Bishop
is consecrated!'

Equally characteristic of the two ladies is their contrasting attitude
to illness and death, topics highly relevant to life in the West Indies
at this time. On Christmas Day 1858 Mrs Rawle wrote:

> There has been so much sickness and death among our acquaint-
> ance, that one had no heart to make much preparation for this
> season.

Mrs Layton, in contrast, had a positive relish for bereavement, con-
soling 'Aunt Harriet' for her sister's death in terms chiming strangely
in the modern ear:

> I think the pleasure of nursing those we love in a last illness is
> exquisite . . . Dear Aunt Margaret would have been very un-
> happy if you had gone before her.

But Mrs Rawle, for all her reticence, was not entirely free from the
Victorian obsession with mortality. Indeed she had little chance of
avoiding it. Mrs Layton tells us that, of Miss Blagg's letters

> . . . there is scarcely one which does not record a death . . . Poor
> Mrs Rawle! How many of her relatives have died since she left
> England on her marriage! I always feel very nervous when the
> packet comes in. Anyone with a large number of relatives must
> expect it to be so. I have worn deep mourning for 22 relations.

In 1858 she records that Mrs Rawle 'is *still* wearing mourning'.
Both ladies write on black-edged paper as often as not, charmingly
ornamented with mourning seals. While Mrs Rawle mourned her
relatives in England, her friends were dying round her in Barbados.
In the year of her arrival she wrote:

> Thier [*sic*] seems to be some fatality all those who have come
> out from England out of nine 4 are dead & one rendered unfit
> for work, now people will say this speaks against the climate
> tho' it will not be quite just.

Even in the much worse conditions in Trinidad, at the height of the yellow fever epidemic of the 1880s, she continued to defend the West Indian climate insisting 'The English climate is *more* trying for old people than this'.

Mrs Rawle's letters from Trinidad are fewer in number but broader in scope than her letters from Codrington. As bishop's wife her horizons were naturally wider. No longer marooned in an isolated rural community, the Rawles now lived with noise and dust drifting in through their windows from the streets of Port-of-Spain, a capital city and port which brought them a constant flow of visitors, mainly from the island's Anglican community, but also from passing officials and notables. Rawle's position as Bishop inevitably brought him into contact with such circles and increased the opportunities for travel which he appears always to have enjoyed – they stayed, for instance, at the Queen's House, Jamaica, as guests of the Governor for the first West Indian Synod in 1885. But in general their way of life seems to have remained essentially unchanged. Its emphasis was still on the remorseless round of Christian duties, though the scale of the enterprise was larger: the parish had become the diocese, the church was transformed into the cathedral. Instead of the College and its schools, there was Trinidad's whole Anglican community, with much the same interplay of personalities, but on a wider and occasionally more dramatic scale, as in the financial scandal leading to the Archdeacon's resignation in 1886. Perhaps the principal difference was that instead of being concentrated, as at Codrington, the community was a scattered one, living side by side with a number of others. There were Chinese and Indians, among whom mission work was carried out, as well as Europeans, each with their own particular brands of Christianity – Roman Catholic and Scottish Presbyterian, for instance, although in religious matters these remained essentially self-contained. Much the same social connotations surrounded these different manifestations of Christianity in Port-of-Spain as elsewhere – the Presbyterian congregation, for example, seems to have been largely a commercial one (there were a good many Scottish shopkeepers in Port-of-Spain), although Mrs Rawle reports the new Chief Justice attending it in the absence of his daughters, who, he expected, would insist on being taken to the Cathedral service.

In their new position of greater dignity, both ecclesiastical and social, the Rawles seem to have remained the same unpretentious, dedicated couple, the 'old man' and the 'old woman' whose working partnership existed to serve their church and its people. Mrs Rawle's letters from Trinidad do contain glimpses of social conditions on the island, eyewitness accounts of the two fires that devastated large sections of Port-of-Spain during the period, references to railway disasters, shipwrecks, the cyclone of 1879, and the epidemic of yellow fever that led to the imposition of quarantine regulations on travel between the islands in 1887. But far more important for the local historian who is interested in what life in Trinidad at this time was actually like, is the picture, emerging almost incidentally from the gossip exchanged with a sister-in-law, of the largely expatriate Anglican community going about its daily business, living, in a Caribbean setting, very much as it would have done in England, and governed by the same set of assumptions. The focus may be narrow and the interest sectional, but there are glimpses of the environment in which, incongruously, this very English, very Victorian community lived.

For the social historian, the letters of Mrs Rawle and Mrs Layton are something of a find, breathing as they do the atmosphere of the period. Their very obsession with daily trivia exemplifies the mental outlook imposed on Victorian women by the restricted atmosphere of their lives. Because Mrs Rawle and Mrs Layton were each in their different ways quite ordinary (though admirable) women, apparently content with the supporting roles allotted to them by society, they faithfully reflect their background. That their particular background happened to be one artificially transplanted to a very different sort of society is an additional bonus.

NOTE ON SOURCES

This article is based on two main sources: the Rawle Papers (MSS W.Ind.s. 41) in the Rhodes House Library, Oxford, and *Bishop Rawle: a Memoir*, by George Mather and Charles John Blagg (London, 1890).

SITING THE CAPITAL
OF THE
CENTRAL AFRICAN FEDERATION

Richard Wood

In all the early schemes for the unification of the Rhodesias, Salisbury was the automatic choice as the capital of the enlarged territory. This was not surprising as Salisbury had no rivals outside Southern Rhodesia, and as most of the early suggestions were for the amalgamation of the territories under the Southern Rhodesian Constitution: the question of an alternate capital did not arise. When federation came to be considered in the post-Second World War era, Southern Rhodesia was deservedly recognized as the senior partner. Not only was she more advanced constitutionally, being a self-governing colony in contrast to her prospective partners, Northern Rhodesia and Nyasaland (which were, as protectorates, ruled directly from Whitehall with limited settler participation in government), but also Southern Rhodesia's earlier and more diverse development meant that she was economically and administratively more sophisticated. Nevertheless, there were now rival claimants to Salisbury and a body of opinion which held that it would be politically expedient to site the capital elsewhere.

In 1896 when the British South Africa Company proposed to place both Rhodesias under the control of its Administrator and Council in Salisbury, the town was the intended capital.[1] But the Jameson Raid shook the trust of the British government which tore up the Order-in-Council it had in preparation. And, though the Company continued in full control of Southern Rhodesia, its role in Northern Rhodesia was reduced to that of supplier and paymaster of the administration, while the British High Commissioner in South Africa governed.

Yet the logic of the situation kept the idea of a territorial merger alive. For example, the British High Commissioner, Lord Selborne, proposed a choice of two schemes in 1907; either British territories south of Lake Tanganyika could federate, or, if that were impossible, Central Northern Rhodesia, encompassing land adjacent to the railway, could amalgamate with Southern Rhodesia, in which case the capital would be Salisbury. Likewise, when the British South Africa Company in 1913–17 renewed its bid to amalgamate the Rhodesias, Salisbury was chosen as the administrative centre much to the dismay of the residents of Northern Rhodesia's capital, Livingstone.

In their greater anxiety to gain responsible government, the Southern Rhodesians proved to be unresponsive and the Company dropped its proposal. But the idea of unification survived this rejection and was proposed again in 1919 by Northern Rhodesian farmers, and thereafter by a variety of individuals and public bodies almost yearly in the inter-war period. Where the unification schemes proposed association with South or East Africa, Salisbury was unlikely to be the capital. But when the amalgamation of the Rhodesias, of the Rhodesias and Nyasaland, or of Central Northern Rhodesia with Southern Rhodesia was advanced, Salisbury was the assumed or stated choice. In 1941 Salisbury housed the Inter-Territorial Council that was created to co-ordinate the territories' war-effort and distribution of essential supplies.

Settler agitation after a conference of Northern and Southern Rhodesian parliamentarians in 1935 prompted the British government to have the problem of the closer association of the Rhodesias and Nyasaland examined by a Royal Commission led by Viscount Bledisloe. Reporting in 1939,[2] this Commission rejected federation as a solution and, because of African resistance to it, would only condone amalgamation as an ultimate objective. Until amalgamation was practicable, the Commission proposed that any inter-territorial co-ordination of services could be effected by a committee chaired by the Governor of Southern Rhodesia and served by representatives of the territories' governments. When the British government implemented this suggestion in 1945, as a sop to the amalgamationists, this ill-fated body, the Central African Council, was also based in Salisbury.

In 1948 the protagonists of amalgamation, and in particular Roy Welensky, the leader of the unofficial members of the Northern Rhodesian Legislative Council, and Sir Godfrey Huggins, Southern Rhodesia's Prime Minister, were brought to the realization that no British government could, in the post-war era, contemplate handing over to a settler-dominated government the control of the destinies of approximately four million Africans in the two Northern protectorates.[3] The consistent rejection of any political association with

Southern Rhodesia by those Africans made such action even more unlikely. The British government had suggested that, if effective inter-territorial co-ordination was essential, executive powers could be given to the Central African Council on the pattern of the East African High Commission. But this was not what Huggins and Welensky were seeking, and the Southern Rhodesian electorate, long-nurtured in the parliamentary tradition, was jealous of its government's independence. Indeed, it had already reviled the Central African Council, although this was a purely advisory body, as a 'Star Chamber Government' which merely presented policy to the territorial legislatures for ratification.

The Northern Rhodesian Europeans, too, were anxiously following moves toward decolonization in the Gold Coast and elsewhere in the Empire and were seeking a means of wresting control of their destiny from the Colonial Office. But in view of the British attitude, the only compromise was to federate in such a manner that an elected federal government could be entirely independent in certain defined fields, such as defence, transport, communications and a score of others, subject to safeguards regarding African interests. The division of subjects, furthermore, would be so arranged that the Federal government would be entirely excluded from any involvement in the Africans' daily life. Indeed the territorial constitutional *status quo* would be maintained. Southern Rhodesia would remain self-governing, albeit with a reduced area of responsibility, and the Northern territories would continue to be protectorates under Colonial Office control. In this manner, it was hoped, African fears of white supremacy would be answered and the co-operation of the British Parliament won.

Huggins persuaded James Griffiths, the Secretary of State for the Colonies, to have this proposal examined at official level[4] and in March 1951 a conference of British and territorial civil servants recommended such a federation. Fearing Afrikaner Nationalist expansionism, Griffiths accepted the need for federation in order to secure a strong British bloc in Central Africa. But he was equally convinced that a federation would not be viable without African support and he proposed to secure it personally. In September 1951 he toured the Northern territories explaining the idea but the Africans were unheeding and a conference at the Victoria Falls at the end of his visit was rendered abortive by the African delegates' refusal to debate the issue. Attlee, too, undermined the Conference when it was barely underway by proroguing Parliament.

The return of the Conservative Party to power in October ended
the period of indecision. The Conservative government agreed that
the need for federation was urgent and in the interests of all inhabitants. It found that African fears were groundless and that their
interests were adequately safeguarded and was prepared, as the
protectorates' trustee, to act. The campaign was hard-fought but
successful. Two constitutional conferences were held, in April 1952
and January 1953. The Southern Rhodesian electorate accepted the
proposal in a referendum in April 1953, and, after ratification by the
territorial legislatures and the British Parliament, the Federation
formally came into being on 3 September 1953.

The Officials' Conference in 1951 produced the framework of what
was to become the Federal Constitution.[5] It designated the subjects
it felt should become federal and devised safeguards for African
interests. It is curious, therefore, that nothing was said on the siting
of the capital when such great care was being taken to allay African
suspicions that federation could be amalgamation by the 'backdoor'
to perpetuate white supremacy. Comment, however, was forth-
coming when the Officials' Report was examined in detail for the
first time at the conference in April 1952. The purpose of this conference was to produce a White Paper outlining definite proposals
for public enlightenment. Acknowledging that the Africans were
likely to equate the Federal with the Southern Rhodesian government, Huggins thought that it should be stated that the Federal
capital need not necessarily be in Southern Rhodesia, and if there,
not automatically in Salisbury.[6] But it might be necessary to create
a small federal state on the Australian pattern. The Conference did
not agree, ruling that it would be wasteful not to exploit the established services of one of the towns even if it would be necessary to
provided housing of which there was a great shortage in the post-war
wave of immigrants. The purely civil-service atmosphere of a Canberra, too, was not attractive. Thus E. C. F. Whitehead, Southern
Rhodesia's Minister of Finance, formally proposed that a federal
or 'extra-territorial' area should be procured within the boundaries
or adjacent to one of the existing territorial capitals. Sir Gilbert
Rennie, Northern Rhodesia's Governor, and V. Fox-Strangways,
the Secretary for Native Affairs in Nyasaland, opined that their
Africans would merely view this as a trick because 'extra-territorial'
would be meaningless to them. Lord Salisbury, the Secretary of
State for Commonwealth Relations, and Welensky thought that

Bulawayo would serve the purpose but Huggins was insistent that the capital had to be nearer the geographical centre of the Federation. The meeting decided that the choice should be left to the Federal Assembly but that the day's press communiqué should make Huggins's point that the capital would not inevitably be in Salisbury or even in Southern Rhodesia.

When the issue was re-debated in the final conference in January 1953,[7] the Southern Rhodesian delegates chose to ignore the Africans' susceptibilities and sought to have Salisbury named as the seat of the Federal government, unless the Federal Assembly decided otherwise. They did not succeed because the Northern Rhodesians were determined to avoid alarming the Africans by giving the impression that the decision was final. Thus Salisbury was named as the Federal capital, provided the Federal Assembly would accept it as such. Otherwise, it would designate an alternative.

Once the territories' fate had been sealed by the Southern Rhodesian referendum in April 1953, Salisbury's rivals emerged. Sinoia, a tiny settlement 80 miles to the north, had a climate equal to Salisbury's and abundant water in the Hunyani River. Marandellas, 45 miles to the south-east, had a marginally better climate. Gwelo sought to be the territorial capital if Salisbury became the Federal.[8] S. N. Hinze, an 'old-timer', suggested Kapese's Kraal on the north bank of the Zambesi, south of Lusaka,[9] where he had prospected in 1904. The Associated Chambers of Commerce and Industry of Northern Rhodesia claimed the capital for their territory because, not only would the Kafue Dam – then to be built before Kariba – remedy current inadequacies of power and water, but African opinion would be placated.[10] Guy van Eeden, a member of the Legislative Council, advanced Lusaka's claim; Chilanga, just to the south, was proposed,[11] but the most strenuous effort came from the Livingstone Municipal Council.

A pamphlet on Livingstone was printed and distributed to the Secretary of State for the Colonies, and to Huggins and Welensky among others. Livingstone's geographical claim was that it was the only town on the border between Northern and Southern Rhodesia.[12] It was equidistant by air from Salisbury, Bulawayo and Lusaka and by rail from the last two. If Bechuanaland joined the Federation, Livingstone would be central and if a corridor to the west coast were secured, it would be at its opening. The town was small but the Zambesi offered limitless water and power supplies as well as unrivalled recreational facilities, and there was suitable land on a ridge overlooking the river where the climate was slightly cooler. Close by, and served by international airlines, was the largest and most modern airport in the three territories. The climate was hot but the land was Crown Land and the money saved on compensation could be spent on air-conditioning. Livingstone, named after the great explorer who had opened the way for the European, was the most appropriate historically. The town was also the oldest European settlement in the territory. Federation would mean the loss of customs clearance business to Livingstone, but the influx of Federal personnel would negate this. Furthermore, the choice of Livingstone would prevent rivalry between the territorial capitals and would allay African fears.

The Northern Rhodesian Municipal Association supported this claim and, after Salisbury had offered a gift of 380 acres at Warren Farm on its western boundary, so did its former mayor, Charles Olley.[13] Olley argued that Salisbury, with 100 000 Africans and 50 000 Europeans, was over-large and would be choked by the Federal civil servants. He feared, too, that the Federal Government's liberal policies would render segregation untenable and provoke an already 'insolent' African population. The choice, however, was the prerogative of the Federal Assembly. Until it was in being, the Interim Federal Cabinet – Huggins (now Viscount Malvern), Welensky and Sir Malcom Barrow of Nyasaland – could do little more than inspect the Warren Hills site, which they found to be excellent. They asked the Southern Rhodesian government to survey it and sought finance for civil service housing from Northern Rhodesia.[14]

As the ability of the Federal government to assume its functions depended on the procurement of office accommodation and civil service housing, it is not surprising that only a week after the Federal Assembly began work in February 1954, Malvern set up a Select Committee to find a capital as quickly as possible.[15] This Committee visited the sites and recommended tersely in early March that the capital should be in or adjacent to Salisbury. In the Federal Assembly on March 8 the Reverend Percy Ibbotson, the Committee's chairman, and his fellow members expanded on their findings.[16] As the criteria had been climate, accessibility, existing facilities, amenities, availability of a suitable site, future development and town planning, water, power and food supplies, relative costs and political considerations, the field had immediately narrowed to Salisbury, Lusaka and Livingstone. Motivated solely by practicalities, the Committee ruled out Livingstone because of its climate. It was acknowledged that there was little to choose between Salisbury and Lusaka. Their climates were similar, both were on the main arterial routes of the Federation, both could easily be supplied with food, and building costs were only marginally cheaper in Salisbury. The deciding factor was that Salisbury had better existing facilities and a dignity which Lusaka, still too new, lacked.

In the debate the Southern Rhodesian European members who spoke, including Ian Douglas Smith, then a member of Malvern's Federal Party, accepted the Committee's verdict on the grounds of practicality and expense. They reasoned it would be more appropriate to use Salisbury's facilities and spend the £7 500 000 to £10 000 000 which would be needed for a capital elsewhere, on hydro-electric power. N. G. Barrett, however, thought Salisbury's facilities could still be exploited to house staff, if there was a fast electric train to a federal capital in Marandellas. The Nyasalanders, P. F. Brereton and the Reverend A. Doig, chose Salisbury. The Northern Rhodesians on the other hand, were divided. Welensky confessed that, for reasons of sentiment, he favoured Livingstone but accepted the Committee's verdict on practical grounds and, in particular, because of the urgent need for accommodation. Van Eeden, a member of the Committee, agreed. But Livingstone's representative, J. C. Graylin, pressed its claim with the support of V. Joyce who saw the bridge at the Victoria Falls as a symbolic link between the territories. Dr A. Scott of Lusaka stated that haste should not be a criterion, because his town's deficiencies could be remedied. It should be the capital, as it was politically more attractive to the African population. The Northern Africans, D. L. Yamba, W. M. Chirwa, C. R. Kumbikano and M. Kakumbi, agreed that the capital should be in the north because Southern Rhodesia's restrictive racial laws made their lives uncomfortable and their tasks as Members of Parliament very difficult. Chirwa, in particular, thought that the federal policy of partnership could not be practised in Salisbury. Salisbury certainly could not inspire as a capital should, and if it was chosen, he feared:[17]

> . . . we are actually building up this Federation on crumbling sand. I do not believe that by choosing Salisbury we are building up this Federation on a permanent foundation.

The Southern Rhodesian Africans who spoke did not entirely

agree. They wanted to be allowed more freedom of movement, but felt that the creation of an extra-territorial area would cushion them from the worst aspects of life in Southern Rhodesia. J. Z. Savanhu thought the Federal presence could have a liberalizing effect on Southern Rhodesia. M. M. Hove would have the capital sited elsewhere in the territory because Salisbury was short of housing. Ibbotson concluded that nothing new had been said as far as his committee was concerned and a vote was taken with 26 votes being cast for Salisbury and 7 against it.

The decision taken, the Federal government found accommodation in central Salisbury. The governments doubled up in rather cramped conditions which were relieved, however, by a building programme – a separate Federal legislature was ready by June 1954 – and by renting offices and purchasing houses in the private sector. There were difficulties, and Government House and King George VI Barracks had to be declared extra-territorial areas to allow liquor to be served to African Members of Parliament and visitors.[18] But by 1959 this was irrelevant because of the reform of Southern Rhodesia's *'petty apartheid'* laws relating to liquor and segregation on transport, in hotels, lavatories and other aspects of public life.[19] Initially there was every intention to develop the Warren Hills site. Members of Parliament visited it, a rival site at Gun Hill was examined and rejected, a report by Sir William Holford – Professor of Town Planning at the University of London – was obtained[20] and options for adjacent land for expansion were secured.[21] However, with great projects such as Kariba pending, ready finance was not available, particularly after a drastic fall in copper prices in 1957. Suggestions were made in the Cabinet that building might begin at Warren Hills through the use of private finance on a hire-purchase basis, but it was found that it was in fact cheaper to do so in central Salisbury.[22] The Warren Hills site was retained, but after 1960 the Federal government was fighting for its life and development there was not considered again.

Several prominent men of the Federal era,[23] reflecting upon the issue, now feel that it was perhaps a psychological error to site the capital in Salisbury – the Northern Rhodesian Europeans certainly resented the boom in Salisbury which resulted from the transfer of the head offices of the copper companies. African suspicions might have been lessened had the capital been sited elsewhere. However, Sir Roy Welensky is adamant that there was no other choice and that it was not even an issue ultimately, because it would have had no effect on the fate of the Federation.[24]

NOTES

1. L. H. Gann, *A History of Northern Rhodesia: Early Days to 1953*, London, 1964, p. 77.
2. Cmd.5949 (1939), Rhodesia-Nyasaland Royal Commission Report.
3. Sir Roy Welensky, *Welensky's 4 000 Days: The Life and Death of the Federation of Rhodesia and Nyasaland*, London, 1964, p. 23.
4. Welensky Papers 6/42 f. 138, Sir Godfrey Huggins to Don Taylor, 5.10.54.
5. Welensky Papers: *Conference on Closer Association in Central Africa*, Vol. III, Report on the Conference, March 1951.
6. Welensky Papers: *Conference on the Proposed Federation of Northern and Southern Rhodesia and Nyasaland, April-May 1952*, Vol. III, Verbatim Report of Proceedings, p. 127, 5 Meeting 28 April 1952.
7. Welensky Papers: C.A.F. (53) *Conference on the Federation of Southern Rhodesia, Northern Rhodesia and Nyasaland*, p. 17. 9 Meeting, 9.1.53.
8. Welensky Papers: 8/56 f. 15, Town Clerk, Gwelo, to Sir Roy Welensky, 3.12.53.
9. Welensky Papers: 8/56 f. 10, S. N. Hinze to Roy Welensky, 17.5.53.
10. Welensky Papers: 8/56 f. 2, D. W. Winchester-Gould to Roy Welensky, 1.6.53.
11. Welensky Papers: 8/56 f. 19, 'A Claim for Chilanga', n.d.
12. Welensky Papers: 8/56 f. 12, 'Livingstone as the Federal Capital of Greater Rhodesia', n.d.
13. Welensky Papers: 8/56 f. 27, Charles Olley to G. E. Wells, A/Clerk of the House of the Federal Assembly, 20.2.54.
14. Welensky Papers: F.G.C. (53) 2 Meeting Minute 10, 30.9.53; 6 Meeting Minute 13, 10.11.53.
15. *Debates of the Federal Assembly*, Vol. I, Col. 82.
16. *Debates of the Federal Assembly*, Vol. I, Col. 841 f.
17. *Debates of the Federal Assembly*, Vol. I, Col. 860.
18. Welensky Papers: F.G.C. (54), 27 Meeting Minute 5, 28.7.54.
19. Welensky Papers: F.G.C. (59), 10 Meeting Minute 4, 19.3.59.
20. Welensky Papers: F.G.C. (55), 1 Meeting Minutes 12, 13, 4.1.55.
21. Welensky Papers: F.G.C. (54), 38 Meeting Minute 2, 11.10.54.
22. Welensky Papers: F.G.C. (57), 27 Meeting Minute 4, 24.7.57.
23. Confidential Interviews with author.
24. Interview with Sir Roy Welensky, 29.8.75.

THE LONG ARM OF SMALL-TOWN ENTERPRISE
Wood, Francis and Chapman – Grahamstown Concessionaires in the Interior 1887–91

Paul Maylam

The discovery of abundant minerals made southern Africa an attractive field for private enterprise in the last thirty-five years of the 19th century. In the scramble to exploit these resources the petty entrepreneur often took his place alongside larger business operations. Both the diamond fields and the Tati gold mines had attracted small-scale speculators in the 1860s. In the late 1880s many concessionaires, excited by the gold discoveries on the Rand, swarmed into the southern African interior to obtain prospecting and mining rights from local chiefs. Some invaded the Tswana chiefdoms of the Bechuanaland Protectorate; others flocked to the kraal of Lobengula, Chief of the Ndebele; others fanned northwards and eastwards into Barotseland, Mashonaland and Gazaland. As at Kimberley and Tati these concessionaires were largely small-scale operators with little capital backing. Often their aim was no more than to be bought out by some larger organization with greater means and more serious intentions.

One such miniature enterprise was a syndicate formed in Grahamstown in March 1887 by three men – Joseph Wood, William Francis and Edward Chapman. Wood was a prominent Eastern Cape figure. Of settler stock, he was a farmer and town councillor, and Albany's representative in the House of Assembly. Francis was a partner in a successful trading business based at Shoshong, the capital of Khama's Ngwato chiefdom. Chapman had also had practical experience in the interior, having travelled widely in Matabeleland in the 1860s.

This syndicate proved to be totally unsuccessful as a business venture: it gained no substantial profit from its activities in the interior. It was significant, however, as a participant in the European scramble for 'southern Zambesia'. Apart from a host of minor concessionaires there were three main parties affected by this scramble: the British government, the British South Africa Company, and local black chiefs – Lobengula and Khama in particular. The Wood, Francis, Chapman syndicate was to become involved with each of these parties. It fell foul of the Imperial government; it haggled with Rhodes and the promoters of the Chartered Company; and it nearly provoked a war between the Ndebele and the Ngwato.

Soon after the syndicate had been formed Wood, Francis and Chapman set out from Grahamstown for the interior in search of a mineral concession. In May 1887 Chapman wrote to Khama asking for permission to prospect in the territory between the Rivers Shashi and Macloutsie, just north of the Limpopo River. Khama refused to grant this permission. The three concession-hunters therefore decided to try their luck with Lobengula. They travelled through Matabeleland and Mashonaland investigating mineral possibilities, but were disappointed when late in October Lobengula refused to grant the syndicate a concession in Mashonaland. The chief did, though, suggest to the group that it might operate in the Shashi-Macloutsie territory. Wood's party therefore journeyed at once to the area where they prospected some ancient gold diggings. Such were their findings that they returned immediately to Lobengula. On 17 November the chief granted the syndicate prospecting and mining rights in the Shashi-Macloutsie territory for an annual rental of £100.

If the concession was easy to obtain, it was far less easy to exploit. The problem was that the Shashi-Macloutsie territory was disputed between Khama and Lobengula. There was no demarcated boundary between the two chiefdoms – the concept of an official boundary was alien to most African peoples. Lobengula, ever grandiose and expansive in outlook, claimed Ndebele overlordship over most neighbouring regions; while Khama was determined to assert his independence from the Ndebele. The disputed Shashi-Macloutsie territory was a test case. Neither side attached economic value to the region; it was important solely for reasons of political authority. Whichever of the two chiefs could exercise effectively his claim to the territory would be strengthening his position against the other.

Khama was furous when he learnt of the concession; and when Wood, Francis and Chapman revisited Shoshong in December he expelled them from his country. Khama had already granted to Frank Johnson and Maurice Heany of the Northern Gold Fields

Exploration Syndicate a mineral concession covering Ngwato country which, in Khama's view, included the 'disputed territory'. There had thus arisen a position where two different groups held similar rights in the same area from two opposed chiefs.

By their subsequent actions Wood, Francis and Chapman seemed to aggravate this potentially dangerous situation. After being rebuffed by the Ngwato Chief they at once wrote to Lobengula saying that Khama claimed the Shashi-Macloutsie territory and that he had prevented them from prospecting there. They also asked Lobengula to send some men down to the Shashi for their protection. They fully realized the implications of the request; 'this may mean war between your people and the Khama's; we should greatly lament anything of the kind, at the same time we want the country you gave us, and intend to work it in terms of our agreement'.

While the syndicate's provocative behaviour infuriated Khama, it also incurred the displeasure of the Imperial authorities. At that time the Rev. J. S. Moffat, the Assistant Commissioner for the Bechuanaland Protectorate, had been mediating between Khama and Lobengula in the hope of bringing them to an amicable arrangement over the 'disputed territory'. The actions of Wood, Francis and Chapman were destroying the possibility of reconciliation. The three men were accordingly threatened with arrest and given a severe warning by the Administrator of Bechuanaland, Sir Sidney Shippard. The Imperial authorities were clearly determined to prevent the recurrence of such disorder and anarchy as had occurred in southern Bechuanaland in the early 1880s when Boer freebooters from the Transvaal exploited divisions between Tswana chiefs to further their own ends.

Wood seems to have soon decided that the best course open to the syndicate was to sell its concession. In Kimberley in March 1888 he met Henry Pauling who was in South Africa investigating commercial prospects on behalf of a Paris-based company owned by Baron Frederic D'Erlanger. Wood authorized Pauling to offer for sale overseas the syndicate's Shashi-Macloutsie concession. So Pauling took back to England for D'Erlanger two options: one for the Shashi-Macloutsie concession, and another for certain farms on the Rand which comprised all the deep level mines of the Robinson and Langlaagte Group. Ironically D'Erlanger rejected the latter option, which would have brought him a fortune, and chose the former, which eventually turned out to be worthless. D'Erlanger agreed to pay £12 000 in cash and £98 000 in shares for the Shashi-Macloutsie concession, but the purchase was conditional upon Lobengula's title to the territory being proved and upon evidence being shown that the Shashi-Macloutsie area did bear gold.

Pauling returned to South Africa in June for the purpose of verifying these two points. In July he met Wood in Grahamstown and the two men travelled to Pretoria. There Wood had interviews with Kruger and Joubert in an attempt to obtain evidence in support of Lobegula's title to the 'disputed territory'. At this point their mission stumbled upon the opposition of the Imperial authorities. While in Pretoria Wood received a telegram from Bower, the Imperial Secretary at Cape Town, warning him not to enter the 'disputed territory'. It was now the policy of the Imperial government to bar all white prospectors from entering the area so as to prevent the Khama-Lobengula territorial dispute escalating into war. Pauling was also told by Bower that no white could prospect in the area till the dispute had been settled. This ban threatened to scotch Wood's deal with D'Erlanger; the purchase of the concession depended upon the territory being proved auriferous, and it was impossible to obtain such proof without prospecting in the area.

Wood and Pauling now decided to visit Lobengula. But again they were thwarted by the imperial authorities. When only sixty miles from Bulawayo they encountered Shippard's party returning to Bechuanaland after discussions with Lobengula. The Administrator warned Wood and Pauling not to proceed further as Matabeleland was 'in a very excited state'. Thereupon the two men accepted Shippard's offer of a safe passage through Bechuanaland. Wood was then sent down to Mafeking where the Acting Administrator, Newton, bound him in the sum of £2 000 not to enter the 'disputed territory'. This humiliating treatment deeply embittered Wood, who was a prominent figure in the Eastern Cape. But it was an effective measure. Wood never again ventured into the interior.

In the meantime Francis and Chapman had pursued a separate course – they seem to have had a dispute with Wood early in 1888. In March of that year Chapman wrote to Lobengula from Grahamstown advising the Chief that he and Francis were again preparing to come to Bulawayo. In June, en route to Lobengula, they revisited Shoshong in defiance of their expulsion order. Khama arrested them and sent them to be dealt with by Shippard. But Chapman escaped from his Ngwato escort, and Francis was released near Molepolole by Setshele, Chief of the Kwena.

They reappeared on the banks of the Limpopo early in July. Bent on punishing Khama, they had proceeded to the Transvaal. There they had recruited a few Boer adventurers and assembled a waggon-load of arms and ammunition. It was this party that a patrol despatched by Khama found on the banks of the Limpopo early on the morning of 7 July. Francis and Chapman were discovered on the northern side of the river – in Ngwato territory. They quickly returned to the Transvaal side on a pont leaving their waggons behind. From the pont Francis was alleged to have shouted threatening words to the Ngwato patrol; 'We have come with the Boers to divide the country', he declared; 'we have an army and we mean to take the country'. Two days later Francis and Chapman and their armed Boer companions – about twenty in number – again crossed the river and successfully retrieved their waggons, the Ngwato patrol retreating. That night the Boers attacked the Ngwato as they were camping down. The Ngwato beat a hasty retreat leaving behind their saddles and blankets, which the attackers burnt – gaining feeble satisfaction for their pent-up aggression.

At about the same time, and not far from the scene of these incidents, another Ngwato patrol had encountered a small Boer expedition led by Piet Grobler, the Sough African Republic's envoy to Lobengula. Grobler was returning from negotiations with the Ndebele Chief when on 8 July his party clashed with some Ngwato sent out by Khama to reconnoitre the 'disputed territory'. During a brief affray Grobler was mortally wounded.

Soon after these events Shippard launched an inquiry into the 'Grobler incident' and into the activities of the Francis-Chapman party on the Limpopo. In both cases he came out strongly against the whites involved in the incidents. He concluded that Grobler had started the one affray by assaulting some of Khama's men. And Shippard was bitter in his condemnation of Francis and Chapman: they had first intrigued, with Wood, to bring about a war between Khama and Lobengula, and then they had led a band of Boer filibusters into Ngwato territory. 'It is difficult', remarked Shippard 'to speak of the conduct of Edward Chapman and William Cecil Francis in terms sufficiently measured to suit the requirements of judicial proceedings or of official correspondence'.

Francis and Chapman avoided arrest by retreating into the Transvaal. But in September they reappeared again – in Matabeleland. They visited Bulawayo to deliver the £100 rental due to Lobengula under the syndicate's Shashi-Macloutsie concession. This Lobengula refused to accept owing to the unsettled state of his dispute with Khama; but the chief did express himself willing to allow the concessionaires access to the Shashi-Macloutsie territory when the dispute was settled.

Francis and Chapman were just two of many white concessionaires and speculators who flocked to Lobengula's kraal in the last quarter of 1888. On 6 October there was a great meeting at the kraal. About thirty white people were present, including Francis and Chapman, and Rudd, Maguire and Thompson who had recently arrived seeking to obtain a concession for Rhodes' great northern enterprise. Two days later Francis and Chapman left the scene of activity. And it was Rudd's party who, late in October, won the cherished prize – a comprehensive mineral concession from Lobengula.

The departure of Francis and Chapman from Matabeleland in October 1888 marked the end of the Grahamstown syndicate's active, physical presence in the interior. Thereafter its operations were confined mainly to bargaining with the Chartered Company, and to pleading with the Imperial government, to permit prospection in the 'disputed territory'.

In March and April 1889 the chairman of the syndicate, T. H. Copeland, appealed to Sir Hercules Robinson, the High Commissioner, to withdraw the ban on Wood, Francis and Chapman working in the 'disputed territory'. But the Imperial government was unyielding in its policy of prohibiting white activity in the area. And so the syndicate soon came to realize that its chances of exploiting its own concession were minimal. It accordingly resolved upon a quick scuttle. Wood had already made a provisional deal with D'Erlanger's company; but that transaction was still in the balance. In 1889 the best course open seemed to be to strike a bargain with Rhodes and the promoters of the Chartered Company. This was the line being adopted by many other concessionaires at this time.

Rhodes had the Rudd concession, but it was not enough. He wanted a total monopoly of European rights in Lobengula's dominions. This necessitated his buying out a host of other concession-holders who claimed to hold rights in the country. And so the

Grahamstown syndicate, like other concession-holders, now began to look to Rhodes rather than Lobengula as the most likely source of profit. Later in the year Wood was negotiating directly with Rhodes in Cape Town. In October Rhodes offered to buy the syndicate's concession for £25 000 and 35 000 shares in a company to float the concession, but he later retracted from the deal. In December Arthur Douglass, another representative of the syndicate, was again negotiating with Rhodes in Kimberley. Typically Rhodes would only make half-hearted offers, keeping his rivals at bay without making any firm commitments.

It was frustrating for these petty entrepreneurs to be treated in this way. Early in 1890 Douglass travelled to London in an attempt to obtain satisfaction for the Grahamstown syndicate. He had interviews with Beit, a director of the Chartered Company, and with Hawksley, the Company's legal representative. An agreement was reached whereby the syndicate was to receive, in exchange for its concession, shares in a company to be promoted by the chartered group for developing the Shashi-Macloutsie territory.

Again it was only a tentative agreement which the Chartered Company had no immediate intention of putting into effect. It had neither the time nor the resources to carry it through; and it was pointless to think of doing so as long as the Imperial prohibition in the 'disputed territory' remained. The agreement was simply a device to keep the 'small fish' at bay. And so Douglass was again in England early in 1891, putting pressure on the Chartered Company to honour its draft agreement. In April a more definite agreement was signed: the Grahamstown syndicate would receive a quarter-share in a £500 000 company which would be incorporated when the imperial government ended its ban on operations in the 'disputed territory'.

The Ndebele War of 1893 and the subsequent death of Lobengula removed the danger of an Ndebele-Ngwato confrontation over the 'disputed territory'. The Imperial ban was accordingly lifted; and in July 1894 the Shashi and Macloutsie Exploration and Mining Company was incorporated. By this time, however, enthusiasm had waned. The high expectations of discovering gold in the interior had been severely dampened by the pronouncements of mining experts. The Shashi-Macloutsie Company petered out like a damp squib. It never carried out mining operations on any scale. The British government's decision in 1895 to place the Shashi-Macloutsie territory in Khama's reserve rendered any such operations impracticable. The strip of territory that had once aroused such wild hopes and enthusiasm remained just another part of the Bechuanaland Protectorate.

Wood, Francis and Chapman never made their fortune; but the syndicate's history does illustrate some leading themes in the European scramble for 'southern Zambesia' in the late 19th century. First, the three Grahamstown concessionaires were typical of many other petty speculators operating in the interior at that time. They were somewhat unscrupulous in their methods, paying little respect to the authority of local rulers. At one point they were even prepared to risk provoking a war between Khama and Lobengula to further their own ends.

Second, the activities of Wood, Francis and Chapman drew a typically cautious reaction from the British government. Imperial policy in the late 19th century was rarely expansionist: it was aimed more towards consolidating the existing Empire and reducing the cost of its administration. Hence it did not support the activities of small-time adventurers who threatened to embroil Britain in costly responsibilities. Rather did the Imperial government try to restrain these adventurers and thereby reduce the possibility of being loaded with new burdens. Hence a firm clamp was placed on Wood, Francis and Chapman.

Third, the later part of the syndicate's history illustrates the way in which Rhodes operated. The syndicate was one of many groups which hoped to gain a share of Rhodes's wealth by presenting its own concession as a bargaining weapon. But Rhodes could not tolerate minor obstructions blocking his path. Sometimes he could force them aside by exercising his influence over certain Imperial officials. At other times he would have to take a more conciliatory approach, perhaps by offering some cash and shares to buy out rival interests. But often these offers were half-hearted and not always honoured. Rhodes's dealings with the Grahamstown syndicate reveal well his strategy of keeping rivals at bay without making too many definite concessions or commitments.

The Wood, Francis, Chapman syndicate had a chequered history. It had started out amidst great enthusiasm; and the syndicate had been an early starter in the great surge of activity in the interior around the late 1830s. It had gone through a period of disgrace, receiving severe reprimands from the Imperial government. For a while it had dared to stand in the way of Rhodes. It finally vanished into oblivion, submerged beneath the larger concerns which came to control the white scramble for 'southern Zambesia'.

NOTE ON SOURCES

This essay is based substantially on correspondence in the Colonial Office Confidential Prints (C.O. 879 series). The most relevant items are the official communications between Imperial representatives in the interior – in particular Sir Sidney Shippard, the Deputy Commissioner for the Bechuanaland Protectorate, and J. S. Moffat, the Assistant Commissioner – and the High Commissioner in Cape Town. These items necessarily reflect the viewpoint of the Imperial administrator who at the time was under instructions to limit Imperial responsibilities and expenditure. Therefore, in this correspondence Wood, Francis and Chapman, whose activities threatened to provoke an inter-tribal war in which Britain might become embroiled, appear in an unfavourable light.

An inside view of the Grahamstown syndicate's activities can be found in two sources. First, there is Wood's own account of the group's travels in the interior and their dealings with Khama and Lobengula between 1887 and 1888, (Joseph Garbett Wood, *Through Matabeleland: the Record of a Ten Months' Trip in an Ox-wagon through Mashonaland and Matabeleland*, Cape Town, 1893, reprinted Bulawayo, 1974). Secondly, the National Archives of Rhodesia hold some of Wood's papers. These are of value mainly because they show how the syndicate attempted to sell its Shashi-Macloutsie concession to Rhodes.

THE GLEN GREY ACT:
Local Origins of an Abortive 'Bill for Africa'

Ruth Edgecombe

In the 1880s and 1890s the Cape liberal tradition of assimilation in racer elations was being eroded by implicit and explicit segregationist legislation. There was a direct correlation between this and the rise of the Afrikaner Bond, growing African political awareness, and the piecemeal annexation by the Cape of the territories between the Kei river and the southern border of Natal, which had large African populations.

The main example of such legislation was the Glen Grey Act, passed in 1894, the year which saw the completion of the Transkeian annexations with the incorporation of Pondoland. Rhodes, the Cape premier, called it a 'Bill for Africa' because, although it applied initially to one district of the Cape Colony, it could be extended 'in whole or in part with such modifications as may be necessary' to the Transkeian Territories and any district of the Cape Colony mainly inhabited by 'aboriginal natives'.[1] In what Rose Innes called 'a flash of vision', Rhodes saw its extension not only to other colonies of South Africa but south and north of the Zambesi and beyond.

The Act was drafted by Cecil Rhodes, and his secretary, Milton, and attempted to deal with the problems of land, labour and the franchise. It reflected a compromise between the views of Bondsmen, on whose support the Rhodes government depended to stay in power, and who wanted the dispersal of the African population, and Cape liberals who wanted to secure African reserves in perpetuity. The Act drew on other 'old ideas' contained in the Reports of the Cape Commission on Native Laws and Customs (1883), the Glen Grey Commission (1892), and the Labour Commission (1893),[2] as well as the views of Transkeian administrators such as Blyth, Brownlee and Stanford.[3] But perhaps the most important shaping factors of this legislation were Bond views on the problems the Act attempted to tackle. These were clearly delineated in letters written between 1891 and 1893 by Victor Sampson, an Eastern Cape farmer and Bond-sponsored candidate for Tembuland in the 1893–4 election, to J. H. Hofmeyr, leader of the Afrikaner Bond.

Sampson saw the location system as the root of the problem of African overpopulation; locations were havens for stock farmers, and in good seasons drew African labour from white farms, spoiling 'the little progress these lazy devils make in the art of manual labour'. The solution lay in giving every existing head of family individual title to a surveyed plot of land and selling what remained to whites. But individual title created the possibility of a very large number of African voters in the long term and this had brought Sampson round to the Bond's view 'that we shall have in this Colony to still further doctor the Franchise as regards the natives'. It was no use raising the franchise qualifications because this would cut off a large number of the poorer white voters.[4]

There should be no restriction on the alienation of individual title because this would only 'perpetuate the vicious location system', and would give the franchise to owners of inalienable land which was quite contrary to Cape constitutional practice. There was no other policy to pursue but to 'liberate' the land so 'that in the course of time it may come into the ordinary market . . .'[5] Both Sampson and Hofmeyr favoured titles to kraals and garden plots only – all other land was to be kept strictly as commonage. The effect would be to 'force the increase of population out of the Transkei to service elsewhere – and thus solve the labour question . . .'.[6] Plots should not be subdivided and should descend to the eldest son. The rest of the family would have to leave the district to seek work. If the commonage were carefully controlled 'we should have cheap labour all over the colony . . .'. Sampson had little hope of being able to persuade Africans to part with their land, but if the 'overgrowth' of population could be forced 'year by year into the labour market', it would be a step in the right direction.[7]

Cape liberals such as J. X. Merriman, James Rose Innes, and J. W. Sauer, favoured individual title, but with restrictions against alienation; and a growing number of Africans favoured individual title.

The spirit of the Glen Grey Act was that '. . . the natives must be treated differently to Europeans . . .'[8] and was based on four premises expressed by Rhodes as

> to give the natives interest in the land, to allow the superior minds amongst them to attend to their local wants, remove the canteens, and give them a stimulus to labour.[9]

The district of Glen Grey, which by 1892 had a population of about 40 000, lay partly in the Queenstown and partly in the Wodehouse divisions of the Cape Colony and consisted of a series of valleys suitable for agriculture and surrounded by high rocky mountains. The grazing in the district was good. The district, which was first occupied by Thembu fugitives from Tshaka in 1827, had a turbulent history of Thembu participation in frontier wars and rebellion against white rule. A Thembu location was proclaimed by Governor Cathcart in 1852, and in 1864 and 1885 only partially successful attempts were made to relocate the inhabitants and colonize the district with white farmers.[10] During the course of time, land in Glen Grey, which had been proclaimed a magisterial district in 1879, was alienated for mission and railway purposes, and to White and African farmers.[11] By 1892, 248 476 of the original 338 014 morgen remained Crown land. Neighbouring white farmers coveted this land and argued that the Thembu had forfeited their rights through war, rebellion and broken agreements. The question of Glen Grey and the wider problems of African labour and land tenure had been matters of parliamentary interest since the 1880s. In 1892 a Commission was appointed to inquire into the Glen Grey lands. The Report of the Commission found that the land did belong to the Thembu; that it was 'only barely sufficient for the use of those at present residing on it'; that there were about $55\frac{1}{2}$ morgen for each family for agricultural and grazing purposes; and that individual title inalienable for three or four years was desirable – limiting land to one family would force the surplus out to labour and prevent the influx of outsiders.[12]

The Glen Grey Act provided for the division of all unalienated land in the district into locations. The locations were surveyed and divided into allotments of about four morgen each to be granted to existing occupiers and other claimants approved by the Governor. No grantee could mortgage his land or in any way pledge his interest in it. The remaining land in each location served as commonage. Grantees had to pay the cost of survey and a perpetual quitrent of fifteen shillings per annum. Alienation and transfer of land were subject to the Governor's approval. There was to be no subletting or subdivision of the land and the principle of 'one man one lot' was to apply. Allotments were to descend by the law of primogeniture and were liable to forfeiture for the grantee's failure to pay the cost of survey or the quitrent for a year; for rebellion; for conviction for theft entailing imprisonment of at least a year; and for failure to occupy the lot beneficially.

The main purpose of the land provision was to fix the existing population on the land. Any increase would subsequently have to go out and work. Rhodes rejected outright the idea of providing more land as a solution to the problem of an enormously increasing population causing overcrowded locations. He refused to insert a provision forbidding alienation of land to whites because it would then become 'a question of class legislation'. The Governor, he claimed, would not allow intermingling and the mission title provided in the Act was basically a 'native title'. It was unthinkable for white men to come and live with their children 'in the midst of savages just emerging from barbarism'.[13]

Clause 26 of the Glen Grey Act aimed at meeting the threat to white voters which was posed by the policy of extending individual tenure where possible, and needs to be seen against the constitutional background. The 1852 Cape Constitution had provided for a colour-blind franchise based on occupation of property, separately or jointly 'with any land', to the value of £25 or a wage qualification of £50 per annum. The franchise was confined to 'natural-born' British subjects, although this condition tended to be overlooked until the controversy surrounding the 1887 Registration Act resulted in a re-examination of the franchise provisions in the Constitution. [14] Those of alien birth had to be naturalized before they could qualify for the vote. Keppel-Jones has suggested that the franchise qualifications were meant to include Coloured rather than African voters. Before the annexations of British Kaffraria (1865) and the Transkei, population percentages in the Cape Colony were approximately as follows: Whites, 37%; Hottentots and Mixed (Cape Coloured), 43%; Africans, 20%. The last mentioned were Caffres and Mfengu who lived in concentrated groups on the eastern frontier. Their political awareness was growing,[15] though relatively few qualified for the franchise. White and Coloured populations were not significantly different in numbers, and in the area within the pre-annexation boundaries, the ratio between them did not change much.[16] After the annexation of British Kaffraria and the Transkei, the racial balance of the colony had shifted as follows: White, 25%; Coloured, 20%; Africans, 55%. Many whites saw themselves as forming 'but a fringe on a vast continent of savagedom'[17] and the Transkeian annexations gave 'a new dimension to the problem of race in

politics'.[18] Between 1882 and 1886, there had been a sharp increase
in African registration on the voters' roll, mainly in the 'frontier'
constituencies.[19] African voters tended to support English-speaking
candidates as opposed to Bond candidates, and as such were a controversial element in Cape politics.[20] The Bond-supported Upington
ministry attempted to deal with the 'native vote' problem at first by
introducing a differential franchise according to colour in the Transkei but these proposals failed to gain sufficient support.[21] In 1887, the
Parliamentary Voters' Registration Act was passed. It discounted
land held under 'tribal or communal' tenure as a qualification for
the franchise. Superficially this appeared to be a measure designed
to exclude the 'red blanket' Transkeian vote, but the words 'or
communal' effectively disfranchised many existing African voters in
the Cape Colony 'proper', where individual tenure had not been
widely adopted among African communities, which tended rather
to hold land on a system that was neither strictly tribal nor individual.[22] There was much opposition to the Act among the English
colonists and Africans, which ensured that the process of registration
would be a subject of intense interest. This was particularly so in
the Glen Grey district where a member of the Bond, T. J. Botha,
brought an action in the Supreme Court to have the voting lists
revised because he claimed that many registered Africans were
unqualified.[23] Botha lost his case, but subsequent petitions from
various people in the Queenstown electoral division, of which Glen
Grey formed a part, prompted the setting up of a Select Committee
to report on the registration lists.[24] The Registration Act resulted in
a significant drop in the number of African voters in areas with large
African populations,[25] but the franchise question was raised again
in the Cape Parliament in 1891 when Hofmeyr claimed that the
Act had not done enough to reduce the threat posed to white voters
by the ever increasing number of African voters. The Franchise and
Ballot Act, of 1892 raised the occupation qualification from £25 to
£75 and required that the prospective voter be able to sign his name
and write his address and occupation.

The Glen Grey Act contained a further attempt to deal with the
supposed threat of the African vote. Glen Grey title would still
count as communal land for franchise purposes. Land held under
tribal or communal tenure in the Transkei and Cape would presumably, when the time came, convert to individual tenure on the Glen
Grey model. Such land, then, could never count towards the franchise

qualification. This might help to explain why the proportion of non-European voters remained at between 15 and 16% of the total Cape electorate between 1892 and 1910,[26] although an African could still qualify for the franchise if he could meet the requirements exclusive of land held under Glen Grey, tribal or communal tenure. Rhodes justified this measure on the grounds that '. . . they were dealing with "citizens" who were children, and as the Government protected their land the natives had no right to claim a vote on it.'[27]

Voters' lists in the district were to be specially revised, quite apart from the usual biennial registration and *Imvo Zabantsundu*, the Xhosa-English newspaper, subsequently referred to reports of the removal of African voters' names from the existing lists.[28]

A further provision of the Glen Grey Act was for local government. Rhodes argued that local affairs should be put before national affairs for 'those children just emerged from barbarism'. Certain chiefs in the Transkei had complained that 'they had nothing to do but grow mealies and think of mischief', that they did not understand concepts of parliamentary rights and racial equality, but they did care about matters of local interest.[29]

Each location was placed under the control of a board of three persons, appointed by the Governor from among the resident landholders. The boards dealt largely with such matters as the prevention of overstocking and the regulation of commonages. The Governor was empowered to establish by proclamation a district council for the administration of local affairs in the district. Six councillors were appointed by him and six were elected by location board members from among themselves. The Resident Magistrate of the district was *ex officio* chairman. The reason for nominating half of the district councillors and having the remaining half elected by men who were themselves Government nominees, was that white farmers were originally intended to be represented on the council. The possibility of an all black council or one with a black majority had to be avoided. The idea of a mixed council was eventually rejected and white farmers were excluded from the system, but the nominee principle remained.[30]

To finance its activities, the Council levied a maximum rate of twopence in the pound on the value of rateable property and an annual minimum rate of five shillings on every registered landholder and every other adult male resident of the district who was fit for labour. Those possessing land under ordinary quitrent title or in freehold were exempt. In this way the Cape government was relieved of local expenditure for the district. The Council was granted local option in matters relating to liquor.

The most controversial feature was the labour tax, stemming as Fairfield in the Colonial Office saw it, from the 'terrible phalanx of Boers Mr. Rhodes has at his back'.[31] All male Africans living in the district and who were judged by the Resident Magistrate to be fit and capable of labour were liable to an annual tax of ten shillings. Those who worked outside the district for at least three months were exempt from the tax for that year. The Resident Magistrate could exempt those who had 'good and sufficient reasons' for staying in the location. Revenue from the labour tax would be used to establish and maintain industrial and agricultural schools in the district – as Rhodes put it, 'the neglect of labour, should provide funds for the instruction of labour', not 'to train up the natives on the basis of Kafir parsons . . .'. The District Council would act as a labour bureau. Rhodes justified the tax with the statement that

> . . . it was the duty of the Government to remove these poor
> children out of their state of sloth and laziness, and give them
> some gentle stimulants to go forth and find out something of
> the dignity of labour.[32]

The large number of Africans in relation to the white minority need not be a cause for anxiety because 'properly directed and properly looked after', they would be 'a great source of assistance and wealth'. If white supremacy were maintained, they would be thankfu lfor Africans 'in their proper position . . .'[33]. If the Glen Grey Act worked successfully, Rhodes planned to abolish locations on private farms and create properly controlled native centres withl abour bureaux.

Criticism in the Cape Parliament turned on details of the measure rather than on the principles involved. Insufficient safeguards against land alienation to whites, the labour tax, the incomplete form of local self-government, the reduction of a man's qualification for the vote, the high cost of survey and the high quitrent, were the main points of contention. There was widespread African opposition to the measure, mobilized to a large extent by Tengo Jabavu, the Mfengu editor of *Imvo*. While individual tenure was favoured, the ease of alienation, the labour tax and the franchise provisions were objected to.[34] Subsequently, because it was decided to extend the provisions of the Act to other districts by request rather than imposition, some of the provisions particularly objected to by Africans were discarded. In 1905, the labour tax, a dead letter almost from its inception, but a 'sentimental' grievance[35] to Africans, was abolished, and land held under Glen Grey tenure was no longer executable for debt. Fears about land alienation proved unwarranted.

Rhodes's vision of a 'Bill for Africa' was not realized, at least not in the form he planned. The land tenure provisions remained largely confined to Glen Grey. They were only cautiously extended to the southern districts of the Transkei and in the 1920s individualization of black-owned land came under official disapproval. The Council system was extended to the Ciskei only after the Native Affairs Act, 1920, had made it permissive for the whole Union of South Africa. By 1932 there were eight local councils which in 1934 were federated in the Ciskeian General Council. Some few local councils were also established in the Transvaal and in Natal, generally without an elective element. Local government in the Orange Free State was confined to reserve boards of management at Witzieshoek and Thaba 'Nchu.

Perhaps the most enduring significance of the Glen Grey Act is that it provided a basis for an experiment in local government in the Transkei which lasted for fifty-five years. The Council system, with some modifications, was extended to four districts in the Transkei in 1894. In 1903, eight districts were added and the Transkeian Territories General Council (the *Bunga*) came into being. By 1928, the Council system extended throughout the Transkei with the exception of the predominantly white Mount Currie district. In 1931 the United Transkeian Territories General Council was formed with the incorporation of the Pondoland General Council (created in 1911). The Council system, which aimed to encourage non-traditional leadership, had, Hammond-Tooke has suggested, potential for effective development if its powers were increased.[36]

But in 1956 the *Bunga* was abolished and replaced with an administrative system 'explicitly based on the traditional chieftainships.'[37] The Bantu Authorities Act of 1951 had provided for the creation of 'homelands' for the various tribal groupings in South Africa, which were to have a measure of self-government and perhaps ultimate autonomy. By virtue of its long experience of local government, the Transkei was the logical starting point for this experiment.

This marked the culmination of the process of separating Africans from 'white' politics in the Cape. The spirit of Glen Grey survived in the Hertzog legislation of 1936, when Africans were removed from the common voters' roll in the Cape, and it achieved its final expression with the institution of the 'homelands' policy, when Africans lost their white representatives elected on a separate roll to the South African Parliament.

NOTES

1. For the full text of the Act see *Cape of Good Hope Government Gazette*, No. 637, 31 August 1894, pp. 1681–93.

2. *Cape House of Assembly Debates* (henceforth *H. A. Deb.*) 2 August 1894, p. 417.

3. E. H. Brookes, *White Rule in S. Africa 1830–1910* (Pietermaritzburg, 1974), p. 79.

4. Hofmeyr Papers, South African Library, Cape Town, Box 15F Native Policy, Sampson to Hofmeyr, 15 June 1891.

5. *Ibid.* Sampson to Hofmeyr, 25 October 1892.

6. *Ibid.* Sampson to Hofmeyr, 3 November 1893.

7. *Ibid.* Sampson to Hofmeyr, 18 July 1893.

8. *H. A. Deb.* 9 August 1894, p. 464.

9. *Ibid.* 26 July 1894, p. 363.

10. Cape Archives. Native Affairs Vol. 215. Papers relating to Glen Grey, statement by Hammond-Tooke, 12 November 1890.

11. Cape Archives. Resident Magistrate, Lady Frere: Letters received 1890–99. Memo on the Tambookie Location.

12. G3-'92. *Cape of Good Hope: Report of the Commission . . . Glen Grey District*, pp. 3–5.

13. *H. A. Deb.* 26 July 1894, pp. 367–8.

14. C. O. 48/514. Sir Hercules Robinson to Sir Henry Holland, no. 151, 31 August 1887.

15. S. Trapido, 'African Divisional Politics in the Cape Colony, 1884–1910', *Journal of African History*, ix, 1(1968), p. 84.

16. A. Keppel-Jones, 'A Case of Minority Rule: The Cape Colony, 1854–1898', in *Canadian Historical Association:* Historical papers presented at Sherbrooke, 8 June 1966; edited by John P. Hersler and Fernand Ouellet.

17. *Cape Mercury*, 2 June 1885.

18. A. Keppel-Jones, *op. cit.*, p. 103.

19. See figures quoted by Sir Gordon Sprigg in the Cape House of Assembly. (*H. A. Deb.*, 15 June 1887, p. 68.)

20. Cf. *Cape Mercury*, 31 March 1887.

21. *H. A. Deb.* 21 April 1886, p. 67; *Cape Legislative Council Debates*, 21 June 1886, p. 265.

22. G4-'83. *Cape of Good Hope Commission on Native Laws and Customs.* Appendix F. Report of the Surveyor-General on the Individual Land Tenure System, 30 July 1881, pp. 373–9.

23. A9–'88. *Proceedings in the case of Theunes Jacobus Botha, Applicant, and Egbert Garcia, William John Hughes and William Edward Wakeford, Respondents.*

24. A19–'88. *Report of the Select Committee on Queen's Town Registration.*

25. *Cape of Good Hope Voters' Lists, 1886, 1887,* (Cape Town, 1886, 1887).

26. Percentages quoted by J. L. McCracken, *The Cape Parliament 1854–1910* (Oxford, 1967), p. 80.

27. *H. A. Deb.,* 26 July 1894, p. 365.

28. *Imvo Zabantsundu,* 14 November 1894.

29. *H. A. Deb.,* 26 July 1894, p. 367.

30. *Ibid.,* 26 July 1894, p. 367; 30 July 1894, p. 379.

31. C. O. 48/524. Minute by E. Fairfield on Loch to Ripon, no. 144, 18 December 1894.

32. *H. A. Deb.,* 26 July 1894, p. 363.

33. *Ibid.,* p. 362.

34. C. O. 48/524. Jabavu to Ripon, 10 September 1894.

35. Cf. Jabavu's evidence, A33–'98 *Report of the Select Committee on the Glen Grey Act,* p. 13, para. 87.

36. W. D. Hammond-Tooke, 'The Transkeian Council System 1895–1955, An Appraisal', *Journal of African History,* ix, 3 (1968), p. 473.

37. *Ibid.,* p. 455.

UITLANDERS IN POLITICS

Andrew Duminy

The position of the Uitlanders in the South African Republic before the outbreak of the Anglo-Boer war has attracted considerable attention. Among the questions which have been asked are whether their grievances were as substantial as they liked to pretend and whether they were united in their opposition to the Kruger regime. Furthermore, it was and is still a common accusation that the war was fought on behalf of capitalist interests and it was a small step from there to the contention that Uitlander politics was itself dominated and manipulated by a group of capitalists.

This essay begins with the assumption that the Uitlander community was divided to an abnormal degree. Gold had been discovered on the Witwatersrand in the late 1880s and the crash of 1890 soon followed. This meant that, before the cyanide process and the development of the deep-level mines promised a degree of permanency to the industry, there were few Uitlanders who concerned themselves with politics; to be 'South African-born' implied a degree of concern about southern African affairs which most immigrants were unlikely to possess. Although the majority of Uitlanders were Britons, a fair percentage were foreigners in whom the rallying-cry 'Flag and Empire' evoked no response.

Johannesburg was a small community and the social set even smaller but it is wrong to assume on this account that a degree of closeness and harmony existed. Small communities are not known for an absence of social division. Apart from the resentment which was likely to be shown by those who had failed to make their fortunes towards those who were the object of their envy, the capitalists were themselves business rivals who were more likely to outwit than co-operate with each other. Elsewhere in the world, labour was intent upon a showdown with capital and there was no reason to believe that the goldmines were – or would long remain – immune from this movement.

In view of this disunity, the question must be asked why it was that on certain occasions the Uitlanders were able to present a united political front.

One answer to this question is that unity was a reaction to the actions of the Kruger government. To some extent, this is probably true. The intransigence of the Transvaal government in the face of many demands – notably the petition for franchise reform which was presented to the Volksraad in July 1895 – must have created a growing feeling of discontent and hostility. The arrogant statement of one Volksraad member that the Uitlanders must fight if they wanted reform convinced many that further constitutional action was pointless. But, while it is possible to argue that this feeling of grievance existed, it would be naïve to conclude that this was sufficient to unite a community or to produce spontaneous collective action. Rather, it created a situation which could be exploited by politicians in their quest for specific goals. It must also be pointed out that, while the Kruger government was widely ridiculed and the object of much resentment, it also displayed considerable skill in playing upon the divisions which existed within the Uitlander community. The anti-capitalist organ, the *Standard and Diggers News*, for example, enjoyed a government subsidy and was suspected of taking political cues from Pretoria.

The first occasion on which Uitlander unity – or the illusion thereof – was created was during the reform crisis of late-1895. The essential strategy then was to subject Kruger to the combined threat of an Uitlander rising and an invasion, in the belief that he would then capitulate to the demands which were set out on December 26th in the Uitlander Manifesto. On December 30th the *Star* commented on the degree of unity which existed in support of these demands, pointing out that even the leading German capitalists and J. B. Robinson's representatives stood behind the Manifesto.

The *Star's* opinion, of course, reflected the editor's own desire to enhance the illusion of unity (F. H. Hamilton had been a member of the Reform Committee which had helped to hatch the plot). It would, however, have been impossible for him to advance such a claim were there a danger of its being disproved by pro-government demonstrations. Doubtless, considerable behind-the-scene efforts had been made by the Reformists to secure the support of key persons. After Jameson's invasion, the entire population was then caught up in the march of events and one of the Reform Committee's first acts was to enlarge its membership so that it could claim to speak on behalf of the Uitlander community as a whole. Following Jameson's capture, a further expansion of the Committee took place, it being hoped that the implication of almost all the leading inhabitants of Johannesburg would create security in numbers.

Apart from these moves, however, there was another means which appears to have been deliberately employed with the intention of creating this spectacle of unity. This was the side-stepping of the Chamber of Mines, many of whose members could not be relied upon for support. Instead, action was taken through the Transvaal National Union, with organized demonstrations of support being obtained from patriotic societies such as the Caledonian Society or from self-appointed groups which claimed to represent Australians, New Zealanders, Natalians or Americans.

The elaborate plans of December 1895 were dashed following Jameson's arrest. Failure aggravated the disunity of the Uitlander community. The members of the Reform Committee squabbled, the Transvaal National Union ceased to exist, and the Chamber of Mines split with the formation of the New Association of Mines, the leading members of which were George Albu, Amandus Brakhan (of A. Goerz and Co.) and J. B. Robinson's Johannesburg representatives. In his *Transvaal from Within*, FitzPatrick described the pessimism which then pervaded Johannesburg. 'Very seldom', he wrote, 'has any community been in a position so unsatisfactory as that in which the people of Johannesburg found themselves in 1896'. They were 'betrayed, deserted, muzzled, helpless, hopeless and divided'.

The members of the Reform Committee were released from imprisonment in 1896 on payment of fines and after they had signed a pledge in terms of which they agreed not to take part in politics. In the case of the ringleaders, the stipulated period was ten years; the others (including FitzPatrick) were silenced until June 1899. Without breaking his pledge, FitzPatrick was able to play a key role in bringing about the reunification of the mining industry, but as far as politics was concerned, there seemed little hope of recovering the ground that had been lost. What little was achieved was the work of leaders who had not played a part in the Reform movement. J. B. Robinson, for example, returned to the Transvaal with the intention of 'settling' the Uitlander question. He found Kruger unyielding and, having learnt this, discovered also through his sponsorship of Schalk Burger in the 1898 presidential election, that it was senseless to hope for support from the burgher electors. A more significant development was the growth of the South African League. This organization, which had been formed after the Jameson Raid to advance the

English-speaking and Imperial cause in South Africa, had at first concentrated on the Cape Colony. After the defeat of the Progressives in the 1898 election, it belatedly recognized that the political centre of gravity had shifted to the North. There, under the leadership of W. D. Wybergh and J. Douglas Forster, it devised new strategies. One was to aid in the defence of Uitlanders as, for example, in the *cause célèbre*, the Edgar shooting case. Another was to petition the Imperial Government for active assistance.

The activities of the South African League by no means evoked unanimous support among the Uitlanders. None of the established Uitlander leaders, apart from George Farrar who was then in London, appears to have been party to the League's plans and the capitalists in general gave it no support. The worth of its strategy was that it created a situation in which the British Government became concerned about the 'loyalty' of the Uitlanders. A most effective device had been discovered whereby Britain, it seemed, could be goaded into greater involvement in the Transvaal's affairs.

This development must be seen against the background of the fresh approach to the South African problem of the new High Commissioner, Sir Alfred Milner. His strategy was not unlike that which had produced the Reform movement in 1895. Again it was believed that, if sufficient pressures were placed upon Kruger, he would capitulate to demands for reform rather than risk war and so lose everything. This meant that, as in 1895, it was again necessary to create a united Uitlander front, not in this instance because Kruger was to be threatened with a rebellion but because the plight of the Uitlanders now became the justification for Imperial action.

The first opportunity to recreate an Uitlander movement of this kind occurred during the 'Great Deal' negotiations of February and March 1899. These arose from an approach by the Pretoria government to Uitlander leaders who had been selected as negotiators by the government itself, it being suggested that all major outstanding points of grievance could be settled. Despite the fact that the government's motives were viewed with suspicion, the negotiations proceeded, FitzPatrick being largely responsible for increasing the number of Uitlanders involved in them. At the suggestion of the British Agent, he also succeeded in focusing attention on the franchise. However, because there was considerable disagreement among the Uitlander leaders on this matter, the proposed five-year retrospective franchise was not included in the main body of the Uitlander reply but was merely tagged on and referred to as 'an expression of opinion' which had been furnished by a sub-committee.

The important thing, FitzPatrick recognized, was that, for the first time since the end of 1895, there was a show of Uitlander unity. Realizing that this front was likely to collapse at any moment in the face of Government threat or bribe, the publication of the Uitlander reply was arranged.

The termination of the Great Deal negotiations coincided with the presentation of the South African League's Petition to the Queen. While the British Government contemplated its reply, it was essential that the illusion of Uitlander unity and popular outrage should be maintained. To meet this need, a new Uitlander organization was formed – the Uitlander Council.

With the principal Uitlander leaders in enforced silence until the three-year term expired at the end of May, the organization of a new movement was extremely difficult. FitzPatrick had secured from Smuts the assurance that, during the Great Deal negotiations, the Government would not act against those who broke their pledges. The fact that the negotiations had been terminated by a breach of faith and that the South African League's petition had now been forwarded to London made such continued forebearance unlikely. It was possible for this reason that the convening of the new council was postponed until June. Alternatively, it may have been feared that disagreements would be revealed in the Uitlander Council which could otherwise be hidden if agitation were confined to preliminary meetings at various places along the Reef. Reports of these meetings, at which motions in support of the Great Deal proposals were passed, were then given publicity in the newspapers over which Milner exercised influence through the Wernher-Beit and Rhodes groups of capitalists, while the British Agent in Pretoria forwarded details of this supposed Uitlander solidarity for transmission to London. It was only on June 10 that the Uitlander Council itself was launched at a mass meeting, convened ostensibly merely to 'acknowledge' the efforts of the High Commission at the Bloemfontein Conference. On this occasion, twenty-four members were elected to represent Johannesburg in the Uitlander 'parliament'.

Milner hoped that, in replying to the Petition, the Home government would seize the opportunity to deliver a clear-cut statement of its demands upon the South African Republic. Instead, commitment to the Uitlander cause was temporarily evaded by means of the proposal for a direct conference between Milner and Kruger at Bloemfontein. Thereafter, events gathered their own momentum and were to lead to the outbreak of war in October.

A major cause of this gathering momentum was the force which was unleashed by the reawakening of Uitlander politics. The impression that Britain was at last adopting a stronger line with Kruger immediately produced increased Uitlander expectations and it was not long before the Uitlander Council showed that it had a will of its own. One of the first acts was to publish a 'Declaration of Rights'. This contained demands which were far stronger than any which had previously been made. In place of the demand for a five-year retrospective franchise which had been attached to the Great Deal reply and which had been repeated at Bloemfontein, it now demanded the franchise after 'one or two' years. An acceptable settlement, it declared, would have to be backed by international compact. Other new requirements included the recognition of English as an official language, the independence of the High Court, the freedom of the Press, the reorganization of the education system and of the entire civil service, and the abolition of all monopolies.

Uitlander demands had, in fact, kept pace with rising hopes. Not surprisingly, when during July and August the Transvaal government began to make offers of concessions, these were rejected in Johannesburg as being totally inadequate. The increased expectations of Johannesburg leaders greatly complicated Britain's position, for unless a settlement were hailed as a great victory in Johannesburg, an enfranchised Uitlander population would be unlikely to influence politics in the South African Republic to Britain's advantage.

As the likelihood of war increased, Uitlanders began to look forward to a new order in which Dutch dominance would be ended and the spoils would be theirs. Long before the first shots were fired, most had fled the Transvaal. The Uitlander Council, created as the mouthpiece for the expression of grievances against the Kruger government, now used its claim to speak on behalf of the Uitlander community in the endeavour to influence the expected peace settlement. FitzPatrick was recalled to Cape Town in 1900, Milner having appealed to him to 'sit on' the former Uitlanders in Cape Town and Johannesburg who were there endeavouring to impose their will upon British policy-makers.

It had been difficult enough to create some semblance of unity among the Uitlanders before the war. After Kruger's government had been removed, the many deep-rooted divisions among the British population of the Transvaal were no longer obscured and political unity in the post-war period proved impossible.

The argument that the Uitlanders were a divided population and that a semblance of unity was created for political purposes implies that this was deliberately done. Who were these politicians who schemed in the background?

The fact that five out of the seven members of the 'Inner Council' which planned the 1895 Reform movement were capitalists can lead to the glib assumption that there was a 'capitalist plot'. What this interpretation overlooks is that there was never any unity among the Johannesburg magnates. During the Reform movement, Robinson's and Goerz's representatives and Albu held aloof. During 1897, the proceedings of the Transvaal government's Industrial Commission of Inquiry and the Government's subsequent failure to implement its recommendations brought about the reunification of the mining industry, but this co-operation did not extend into politics. When Wybergh became president of the South African League, he was forced to end his association with the Consolidated Gold Fields. During the Great Deal negotiations, E. Birkenruth (of Consolidated Gold Fields), J. M. Pierce (the manager of the Robinson Bank), H. F. E. Pistorius (the manager of E. W. Tarry and Co.), Georges Rouliot (of the Corner House) and Brakhan were the members of the Johannesburg committee with which the government representatives negotiated. None of these individuals was active in politics and doubtless it was their disinterest which commended them to the government when it chose them to speak on behalf of the Uitlander community. After Rouliot had consulted FitzPatrick, he became party to the scheme to widen the scope of the negotiations, but it was with the utmost difficulty that the others were persuaded to do this and Brakhan finally refused to commit himself to a five-year retrospective franchise.

Initiatives, in fact, lay with the Transvaal government in its dealings with the capitalists. It was easy to sow mischief between business rivals, particularly when many held, or competed for, state monopolies or other favours. The offer to settle the *bcwaarplaatsen* dispute as part of the 'Great Deal' was a very tempting one, for it would enable mine-owners to obtain the mineral rights on the land adjoining their mines, where it had been found that the reefs extended at the deeper levels. Hardened businessmen are unlikely to upset the stability which enables them to prosper. It is therefore a mistake to assume that the demonstrations of loyalty which many of the Rand-lords displayed once war had been declared proved their support for the Imperial policies which had produced the war. It is an interesting fact that in April 1899 at the very time when FitzPatrick was engaged in working up support for a five-year retrospective franchise, J. Emrys Evans, the British Vice-Consul in Johannesburg, wrote to Milner to inform him of the general apathy of the 'better classes' in Johannesburg. 'Frieddie' Eckstein had told him that the Corner House (the firm with which FitzPatrick was associated) was about to make its peace with the government, having been 'brought to their knees' by the proposal to allow public tenders for the *bewaar-plaatsen* rights.[1] In May 1899 one of the leading capitalists (repre-senting A. Dunkelsbuhler and Co.) gave expression to what must have been a common feeling when he exclaimed: 'How I wish there was no politics and one could be left to make money in peace!'[2]

FitzPatrick left Johannesburg in May 1899, having been urged by Milner to go to England and attempt to influence the British Press. It is hardly surprising that, after his departure, when the Uitlander Council was launched, the lead had been taken by 'non-capitalists' such as H. C. Hull, W. Hosken, J. W. Quinn and the leaders of the South African League. Of the 48 members of the Council, only six were mining capitalists or were connected with the large mining houses. Dalrymple was George Farrar's manager in Johannesburg. Samuel Evans and H. A. Rogers were associated with the Corner House, while D. J. Pottinger, W. St J. Carr and H. S. Caldecott were themselves financiers with interests in the mining industry. Con-spicuously absent are representatives of the other major financial houses such as the Consolidated Gold Fields, Barnato Brothers, Neumanns, Albus Goerz and Co. or Robinsons. Whatever these facts reveal, it is not a capitalist interest in politics, nor a concerted attempt by them to dictate policy. Furthermore, in view of the fact that the Uitlander Council included labour representatives such as T. R. Dodd, A. S. Raitt, and C. D. Webb, the capitalist representa-tion did not even suggest a common determination to *defend* its interests.

The activities of *some* capitalists in politics fall very far short of a conspiracy. Apart from the activities of Robinson during 1897 and of Farrar who retained an interest in Transvaal affairs even though he was then exiled in London, the capitalist who was most active in

Transvaal politics was FitzPatrick. But FitzPatrick, although he became a partner in the Corner House, was not a wealthy magnate. Nor did he engage in politics on behalf of his superiors, who were in fact extremely nervous about his political obsession. Time and again he found it necessary to reassure them that he would do nothing which threatened the interests of the firm. In 1906 he was eventually to sever his connection with the firm altogether after Beit had told him bluntly that he was an embarrassment. For him political considerations took precedence over business interests. In this respect he differed from almost all his capitalist colleagues.

NOTES

1. J. E. Evans to Milner, 19th May 1899, Milner Papers, vol. 12(10))
2. FitzPatrick to J. Wernher, 8th May 1899, FitzPatrick Papers A/LC VII.

NOTE ON SOURCES

The theory that the Anglo-Boer war was fought on behalf of Capitalist interests was expounded by J. A. Hobson in his book *The War in South Africa, Its Causes and Effects*, London, 1900. More recently, A. Atmore and S. Marks ('The Imperial Factor in South Africa in the Nineteenth Century: Towards a Reassessment', *Journal of Imperial and Commonwealth History*, III, 1, 1974, 105–139) have renewed debate by contending that due emphasis should be given to the gold and monetary crisis of the 1890s as a 'factor' in Britain's South Africa Policy.

The 'capitalist conspiracy' was transferred from imperial policy into Transvaal politics itself by G. Blainey in his article, 'Lost Causes of the Jameson Raid', *Economic History Review*, 2nd Series, XVIII, 1965, (350–66). Since then, Blainey's assumptions regarding the Reform Plot have been questioned (see R. V. Kubicek, 'The Randlords in 1895: A Reassessment', *Journal of British Studies*, XI, 2, 1972, 84–103). However, an in-depth study of Uitlander politics in the ensuing three and a half years by A. Jeeves ('The Rand Capitalists in Transvaal Politics, 1892-9', Ph.D. Queen's (Canada) 1970) argues that by early 1899, 'the magnates' had again been drawn into concerted political action.

This essay, which advances the alternative interpretation that there was never any capitalist political solidarity – even amongst the 'deep-levellers' – is based upon a study of one of the leading Capitalist politicians (A. H. Duminy, 'The Political Career of Sir Percy FitzPatrick,' 1895-1906, Ph.D. Natal, 1973).